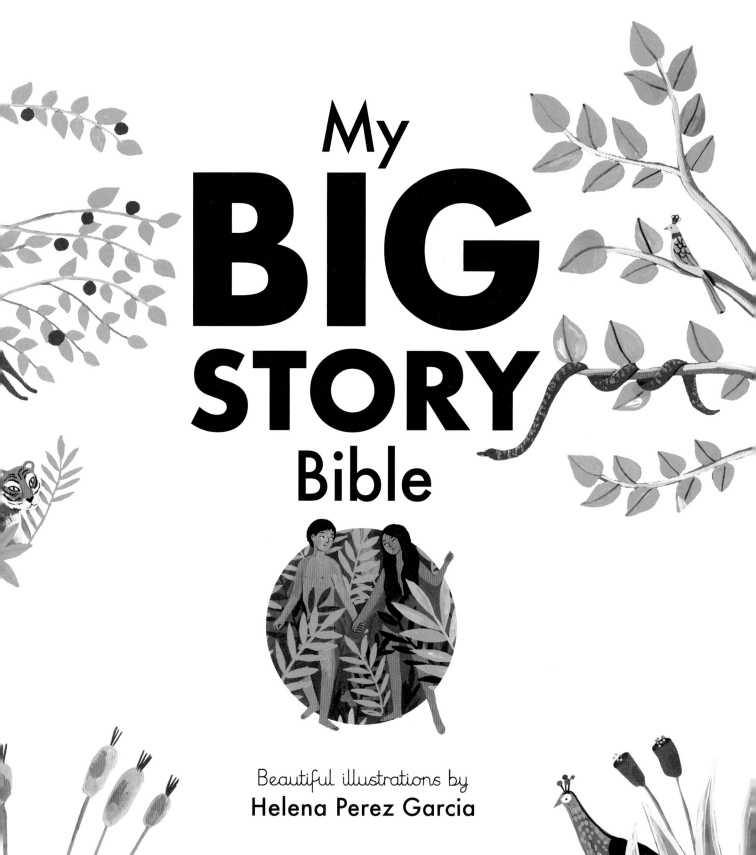

# My BIG STORY Bible

Beautiful illustrations by
Helena Perez Garcia

# TOM WRIGHT

First published in Great Britain in 2024 by SPCK

SPCK
SPCK Group
Studio 101
The Record Hall
16–16A Baldwin's Gardens
London EC1N 7RJ

www.spck.org.uk

British Library Cataloguing-in-Publication Data

A catalogue record for this book is available from the British Library

ISBN 978–0–281–08561–3

1 3 5 7 9 10 8 6 4 2

Typeset by Viki Ottewill
First printed in China by Leo Paper Group
Subsequently digitally printed in Great Britain
Produced on paper from sustainable forests

# Contents

# Part Two

## God's Story in the New Testament

## Maps

# Introduction

I was excited to be asked to put this book together because I have often felt that too many children's Bibles don't present the whole story. They sample little bits from the Old Testament, and maybe slightly more from the New Testament, but without any sense of how the whole great drama really works. I'm talking about the big story that the Bible gives us of God's rescue plan for the world, focused of course on the story of Jesus, but going right back to the beginning of creation in Genesis and right through to the climax of the new creation at the end of Revelation.

One reason I was eager to write this book is that I now have grandchildren, and as I watch them grow up and see how they respond to stories, whether in church or at home, I notice many things that I don't think they're quite getting. I'd like to make available to them key points which, over the many years that I've been studying the Bible, have become very important to me.

Over my lifetime I have become aware that many Christians imagine that the Bible story is simply about Jesus, and that thanks to him we can go to heaven when we die. But then when you look back at the Old Testament, you find you're left with lots of stories which may have a little moral lesson for us, but not much more. The result is that much of the Bible can become a sort of Christian version of Aesop's fables. The problem with that approach is that it fails to convey the big story about God to which all the little stories contribute: the big story of the world in which God wants to come and be at home with us, his human creatures. This is the story which the Bible tells from Genesis onwards, focused of course on Jesus, the Word made flesh, and his saving death and resurrection.

I'm thinking particularly of the time when God was present with his people in the tabernacle in the wilderness and the Temple in Jerusalem, then when God came to live among us in Jesus and the Spirit, and finally, in those wonderful words at the end of the Bible, the time when "God has come to dwell with humans!" (Revelation 21.3). Those are all vital elements of the big story that need to be told again and again. I was eager to find ways of telling it visually as well as in words. I hope you and your children or grandchildren, nieces and nephews, and all who read this book, will enjoy the 140 stories gathered here. I also hope you'll enjoy exploring the many links between the stories and the way that together they build into the one big story about God's plan to make the world his home and to bring heaven and earth back together at last.

# Part One

God's Story in the Old Testament

# God Creates the World

Where's this in the Bible?

Genesis 1

In the beginning God created heaven and earth. God's Spirit was moving over the dark empty waters that swirled around the earth. God spoke, and at his word a bright dazzling light scattered the darkness. Then God spoke to the waters. Some of them became the sea, and some became clouds in the sky. God spoke again, and masses of land rose up out of the sea: huge continents and little islands, mountains, hills, and valleys. Then God covered the land with plants: trees, bushes, grasses, herbs, and bright, beautiful flowers.

Next, God made the warm beams of the sun to shine through the clouds. The sun gave light to the earth in the daytime, and at night the earth's moon and millions of stars lit up the sky.

Then God decided to make living, breathing creatures. First, he made creatures that live in the water: smooth animals that swim, dive, glisten, and spurt. Then God made creatures that fly in the air: feathery animals that glide, swoop, twitter, and squawk. Then God made creatures that live on land: furry animals that run, jump, squeak, and roar. God also made little creatures that crawl, scuttle, spin, and buzz.

God looked at everything in the world, and it was all good. But God knew it needed something more. He wanted all the plants and animals to be looked after. So, last of all, God created humans. He made them to be like him. "Become a great family," said God. "Look after my world!"

God saw it all. It was very good. The work was done. God came to settle down in the world he had made. He was at home.

What else in God's big story links up with this?

**The Promise of a New World**
p. 132

THE OLD TESTAMENT

# The Garden of Eden

Where's this
in the Bible?

Genesis 2

When God created the world, he decided to make a garden. It was called the Garden of Eden. Out of the garden flowed a river that turned into four great rivers, watering the earth. God gave the garden to the first man to look after. It was the most beautiful garden you could imagine. It was how God wanted the whole world to be.

The garden had every kind of tree, including two special ones. One was called "the Tree of Life". If anyone ate its fruit they would live forever. The other tree was called "the Tree of Knowing Good and Evil". God told the man that he mustn't eat from that tree. To snatch the fruit and eat it now would mean going against God. And that would mean death.

God showed the man all the animals he had made. The man gave them names. But none of the animals was really like him, and the man felt lonely. So, while the man was in a deep sleep, God took part of the man and made him a partner.

When the man awoke, he could hardly believe his eyes! Now he had a companion, just like him: someone to love, someone to share his life, someone to help him care for God's garden. The man called his partner "woman".

The man and the woman were naked, but it didn't matter. They had nothing to hide from God.

What else in God's big story
links up with this?

**New Heaven,
New Earth**
p. 280

# What are Humans?

Where's this in the Bible?

Psalm 8

*This poem is from the book of Psalms. The poet gives praise and thanks to God for creating the world and helping humans to look after it.*

God, the Lord, is great and mighty,
All creation sings his song.
Even little children praise him,
Shaming everything that's wrong.

When we gaze on stars and planets
Sometimes we are bound to ask
Why does God think us so special?
What are humans? What's our task?

Yes, we're small, much less than angels,
But we're made to share God's reign,
Caring for his whole creation,
Looking after his domain.

Sheep and oxen, all the creatures,
Birds and fishes, great and small,
We are there to help them flourish,
Caring wisely for them all.

God, the Lord, is great and mighty,
All creation sings his song.
All the earth proclaims his glory,
We will praise him all day long!

What else in God's big story links up with this?

**Jesus, the New Beginning**
p. 282

# The World Goes Wrong

Where's this in the Bible?

Genesis 3

In God's garden there lived all kinds of animals. One day, a crafty snake slithered up to the woman and asked her a question: "Did God really say you mustn't eat the fruit from the Tree of Knowing Good and Evil? Why would God say that? Could it be because God knows that if you eat it you will become wise, like him?"

The woman looked at the tree and thought she might like to be wise. So she reached up and picked some of the fruit. How delicious it tasted! Then she gave some to the man, and suddenly they both knew that something was wrong. They looked at each other and felt ashamed. Quickly, they covered themselves with leaves and hid behind some bushes.

That evening, as usual, God visited the garden. "Why are you hiding?" asked God.
"Because we're naked," replied the man.
"How did you know?" asked God. "Did you eat from that tree?"
The man pointed to the woman. "It was her fault," he said.
The woman shook her head. "No!" she protested. "It was the snake's fault."

God had wanted the man and woman to trust him. He was sad that they had listened to the crafty snake. He was sad, too, when they tried to blame each other. So, with a heavy heart, God told them that they would have to leave the garden. From now on they would be exiles: people who could no longer live in the place where they really belonged. An angel with a flaming sword would guard the garden gate. Life would become hard, and the world would be dangerous.

God also had something to say to the snake. It would be the lowest of all the animals, and one day a special child would be born who would fight the snake. The child would win the fight and put right everything that had gone wrong.

What else in God's big story links up with this?

**Exile!**
p. 112

**Jesus Goes into the Desert**
p. 150

# Cain and Abel

Where's this in the Bible?

Genesis 4

The man God had created was called Adam, and the woman's name was Eve. They were sorry to leave the Garden of Eden, but they still found beauty and wonder in the world outside. At last they found somewhere to settle and start a family. Eve gave birth to two sons: Cain and Abel. When they grew up, Abel looked after sheep, while Cain worked on the land.

For a long time they lived and worked together as brothers, but then one day something terrible happened. The two brothers wanted to give something to God. Cain gave something he had grown in the fields, but Abel gave the best of his animals. God was pleased with Abel's gift, but not with Cain's. That made Cain very angry.

"Why are you angry?" asked God. "Watch out! Something bad is lying in wait. It's out to get you." But Cain didn't listen to God. Instead, he let his anger grow inside him, until, one dark and dreadful day, his anger became so strong that he murdered his brother in a fit of rage.

"Where is Abel, your brother?" asked God.

Cain looked anxious and ashamed. "How would I know?" he said. "Am I supposed to look after my brother?"

But God knew what had happened. He told Cain that from then on the ground would be his enemy. He would have to leave God's presence. So off he went, far away from God. Cain made his home in the land of Nod, east of Eden. There he got married, had children, and built a city. Some of Cain's children became musicians. Others made things from metal.

Adam and Eve were very sad to lose Abel. For a long time they mourned for him, but later they had another son. His name was Seth.

# Noah and the Big Flood

Where's this in the Bible?

Genesis 6–8

Time passed, and more and more humans were born. After many years, the earth was full of people. But they didn't care about God. Instead of loving God, they turned away from him, and they were selfish, mean, and cruel to one another. God was sorry he had made them. So he decided to start again.

But there was one person who loved God. His name was Noah. God told Noah and his family to build an enormous boat. Then, when the boat was ready, God told them to bring into it a pair of every kind of animal, male and female. What a task! It was hard work building such a big boat, and when it was finished it took a long time for the animals to climb aboard, but at last they were all inside.

That was when it started to rain. It rained and rained, non-stop, for 40 days and 40 nights, until the whole earth was covered in water. Everything was drowned except Noah and his family, and the animals who were safe inside the big boat.

When the rain stopped, God sent a wind to dry up the water. But the boat was still floating, and Noah wanted to know when it would reach dry land. So he sent a raven up into the sky to see what it could find. But the raven just flew back and forth. Then Noah sent a dove. Off it flew, but it returned with nothing. He sent it out again, and it flew back with a fresh olive leaf in its beak. "That's good," said Noah, "the earth is coming back to life!" Noah sent the dove out again, and this time it didn't come back.

At last, the flood dried up. Noah, his family, and all the animals came out of the boat and into a bright new world. They all praised God, and God promised never to flood the earth again.

As a sign of his promise, God placed a rainbow in the sky.

THE OLD TESTAMENT

# The Giant Tower

Where's this in the Bible?

Genesis 11

After the flood, Noah's children and grandchildren started to look for new places to live. But they didn't want to be scattered over the earth. They wanted to be together in one place.

"Hey! Why don't we build a big city?" they said. "And in the middle let's build a giant tower!" So that's what they did. They thought their tower would reach all the way from earth to heaven. They thought they were very clever.

God came down to have a look. He saw how proud the people were of their tower. He saw how they wanted to do everything without him. That made him sad.

God decided something had to change. In those days, the world had just one language, so instead of allowing everyone to speak the same language, God made them speak lots of different ones.

When that happened, the people building the tower didn't feel so clever. They tried to talk to one another, but it was no good. Some tried shouting orders. They shouted and shouted, and waved their arms about, but nobody could understand them! In the end they threw down their tools and gave up.

The people left the tower half-finished and wandered off to look for other places to live. So they ended up scattered over the earth after all.

The place where they tried to build the tower was called Babel, because of the babble made by all the languages.

What else in God's big story links up with this?

**Jesus Sends
God's Holy Spirit**
p. 230

# God Calls Abram

Where's this in the Bible?

Genesis 12, 15

A long time after the flood, when the tower of Babel was just a distant memory, a man called Abram lived in a place called Haran. God said to Abram, "Leave this place, and I will show you where to go. I will lead you to a new land and make you the father of a great nation. I will bless you, and through you I will bless all the families in the whole world."

Abram wasn't sure what this meant, but he and his wife decided to obey God's call. They got their servants to pack everything up for their journey, and then they went on their way. Many long days later, and hundreds of miles from where they started, they reached the land of Canaan. "This is it!" said God. "This is the land I have promised to give you. This is the Promised Land."

Abram found a good place to stop and make camp. Then he found some large stones and piled them up to mark the places where he would pray and worship God. The piles of stones were called altars.

One day, as Abram looked out over the land, God himself appeared to him. God told Abram that everything he could see would be for his family and for all the families that came after them. Then, one night, God told him to look up at the sky. Abram looked up and saw that the sky was sparkling with millions and millions of stars. "Look at all the stars," said God. "That's how many children you will have."

Abram believed what God had promised. He had faith that God would keep his promise. God had made Abram his partner.

What else in God's big story links up with this?

**Paul Explains
God's Plan**
p. 260

# God Makes a Special Agreement

Where's this
in the Bible?

Genesis 17, 18, 21

Abram was puzzled. God had promised that he and his wife would have lots of children. But surely God must know that they were far too old for that to happen! How could God's promise come true?

God wanted to help Abram understand that the promise really would come true. So God decided to make a special agreement. The special agreement said that God would give Abram a great land for his children and grandchildren. Those grandchildren would have lots more children. Then so would they, and so would they, until there were so many children they would become a whole nation.

As part of his special agreement, God changed Abram's name to "Abraham", which means "father of many nations".

The years went by. Soon Abraham would be 100 years old, and his wife, Sarah, would be 90. But still they had no children. The thought of becoming a father at 100 made Abraham laugh. Then, one day, three mysterious visitors arrived at Abraham's tent. Abraham invited them to stay and share a meal, and while they were eating one of them said, "This time next year, Sarah will have a son." Now it was Sarah who laughed.

But a year later, God's promise came true. Sarah gave birth to a son. They named him Isaac, which means "laughing one".

What else in God's big story
links up with this?

**Paul Explains
God's Plan**
p. 260

# The Boy Who Nearly Died

Where's this
in the Bible?

Genesis 22

Isaac grew to be a fine strong boy, and Abraham loved him dearly. One day God said to Abraham, "I want you to take Isaac to the top of a mountain and offer him to me as a sacrifice." (To sacrifice something means to give it up. Sometimes this means giving up something precious that you dearly love.) Abraham was puzzled. After all those years of waiting for God's promise to come true, why was God now telling him to do this? Could it be that God wanted to see how much Abraham really trusted him?

That night, Abraham was so worried that he hardly slept. But the next day he got up early and did as God had said. He woke Isaac and together they set off toward the mountain. Isaac had gone with his father on a journey like this before. At the end of the journey, he had watched while his father built an altar and sacrificed a lamb by killing it and offering it to God. After building the altar, Abraham would put some firewood on the top, and then he would kill the lamb and place it on the wood. But now Isaac was puzzled. His father had given him the wood to carry, but where was the lamb for the sacrifice?

When they reached the top of the mountain, Isaac helped his father build the altar. Then Isaac put the firewood on top, while Abraham, tears running down his face, got ready to sacrifice his son.

Suddenly, Abraham heard God's voice: "Abraham, stop!"

Abraham froze. "Now I know you really trust me," said God. And at that moment Abraham saw a goat with its horns caught in a bush. He took the goat and sacrificed it instead of Isaac.

Then Abraham put his arms around his son, and together they walked back down the mountain.

What else in God's big story
links up with this?

**The Journey to
the Cross**
p. 214

# A Wife for Isaac

Where's this
in the Bible?

Genesis 24

When Isaac had grown into a man, and his mother Sarah had died, Abraham decided it was time for Isaac to get married. So Abraham called one of his servants and gave him a special job. "Go to my family who are still living in Haran," said Abraham, "and there you will find the young woman who will marry my son."

The servant climbed onto his camel and made the long journey. When he was near the town of Haran, he stopped next to a well. There he prayed to God. How would he know who would be the wife for Isaac?

Just then, he saw a young woman called Rebekah coming out to fetch water from the well. It was a hot day in a hot country. Rebekah gave Abraham's servant a drink, and his camels too. The servant could see that Rebekah was both beautiful and kind. Surely, she must be the one!

Rebekah took the servant back to her house, where she lived with her brother. His name was Laban. When the servant told them why Abraham had sent him, Laban said, "Here is Rebekah. She will be a fine wife for Isaac."

So Rebekah went back with Abraham's servant to the land of Canaan. As soon as Isaac saw Rebekah he knew he loved her, and she became his wife.

# Jacob Tricks His Father

Where's this in the Bible?

Genesis 25, 27

Rebekah was expecting a baby, and it turned out to be twins. They were called Esau and Jacob. When they were born, Esau came out first and then Jacob followed straight after, gripping his brother's heel. When they grew up, Esau became a hunter, while Jacob preferred to stay at home, where he would often help with the cooking.

A long time later, when Isaac was old and going blind, he asked Esau to go out and hunt for the kind of food he loved. "Then," said Isaac, "I will give you my blessing." (In those days, a father would bless his eldest son by promising to leave him everything, including all his land, after he had died.)

But Rebekah had other plans. As soon as she heard what Isaac said to Esau, she found Jacob and gave him these instructions. "Quick!" she said. "While your brother is out hunting, cover your shoulders in these animal skins while I go and cook a lovely meal for your father."

At first, Jacob was puzzled, but then he understood. Esau's skin was much hairier than his, so with these animal skins covering up his own smooth skin, Jacob would feel, and even smell, like Esau.

Jacob did as his mother told him, and when the meal was ready he took it to his father. When Isaac had finished eating, he stretched out his arms and placed his hands on Jacob's hairy shoulders. Then Isaac gave Jacob his blessing, believing him to be Esau. The trick had worked!

When Esau found out what had happened, he flew into a rage. It was time for Jacob to leave home in a hurry.

# The Stairway from Earth to Heaven

Where's this in the Bible? Genesis 28–32

Jacob ran. He knew he had to leave, but where could he go? He decided he would look for Laban, his uncle who lived in Haran, and tell him what had happened.

It was a long journey. One night, he was so tired that he went to sleep with a stone for his pillow. As he slept, God sent him a dream. In the dream he saw a stairway that stretched from earth to heaven. Angels were walking up and down on it. And there, standing at the top, was God. "I am with you," said God. "This land is for you and your children, and you will be a blessing to the whole world." When Jacob woke up, he said to himself, "This place must be the House of God!"

At last Jacob arrived in Haran, where he found Laban and the rest of Abraham's family. Jacob stayed with them for seven years, working on Laban's farm. During that time, Jacob fell in love with Laban's younger daughter, Rachel, and he asked to marry her. But Laban tricked Jacob and gave him his elder daughter, Leah, instead. Laban then promised to give him Rachel as well, if Jacob promised to work for him for another seven years.

After those seven years had gone by, Jacob decided to make the long journey back to Canaan. He gathered his two wives, his large family, and all their belongings, and they set off. One night, something very strange happened. Jacob was alone outside, when suddenly he met a stranger who challenged him to a wrestling match! All through the night they wrestled, and in the morning Jacob realized that the stranger was an angel. The angel gave him God's blessing. "You know, Jacob," he said, "you should really be called 'Israel'." The name Israel means "fighter of God".

What else in God's big story links up with this?

**The Wonderful Temple**
p. 92

**A Song for Everyone!**
p. 278

# Joseph the Slave

Where's this in the Bible?

Genesis 37, 39

Jacob continued his journey back to Canaan and settled there with his family. By now he had 12 sons. Jacob was proud of them all, but there was one son who made him especially happy. His name was Joseph. Jacob spoiled Joseph and gave him a special coat. Joseph's brothers thought Jacob loved Joseph more than them, and they were filled with envy.

Joseph had amazing dreams. In one, it was harvest-time and each brother's bundle of corn bowed down before Joseph's. In another, the sun and moon and 11 stars were bowing down to him. Joseph's brothers hated him when he told them his dreams.

Jacob had lots of sheep and goats, and his sons helped to look after them. One day, Jacob sent Joseph out to the fields to see how his brothers were getting on. The brothers saw him in the distance. Some of them hated him so much they wanted to kill him. But Reuben, the eldest son, said no. So instead, they grabbed Joseph and threw him into a pit. The brothers were wondering what to do with him when they saw some strangers riding toward them on camels. That gave them an idea. They lifted Joseph out of the pit and sold him to the strangers. Then they went home. But what would they tell their father? They decided to say that Joseph had been killed by a wild animal.

Meanwhile, tied to a camel, Joseph was being dragged away, miles and miles from his home and family. He was only a boy, and he was scared. Where were the strangers taking him? At last, they arrived in the land of Egypt, where the strangers sold him as a slave to a man called Potiphar. Potiphar was a soldier who worked for Pharaoh, the king of Egypt. Although Joseph was scared, he knew God was with him. Joseph worked hard for Potiphar, who was so pleased with him that he put him in charge of everything in his house.

What else in God's big story links up with this?

**Exile!**
p. 112

# Joseph the Great Leader

Where's this in the Bible?

Genesis 39–45

Joseph grew into a handsome young man. One day, Potiphar's wife found Joseph and tried to get him to go to bed with her. But Joseph said no. At this, she became so angry that she pretended Joseph had attacked her. Potiphar believed her and put Joseph in prison. While he was there, he made friends with two other prisoners. They both had strange dreams, and they were amazed when Joseph told them what they meant.

Years later, Pharaoh himself had some dreams, and wanted to know their meaning. Someone told him about Joseph, so he sent some guards to fetch him from the prison. Joseph knelt before the throne. "This is what I dreamed," said Pharaoh. "Seven thin cows ate up seven fat cows but the thin cows were still just as thin as before. What does it mean?" So Joseph explained the dream. "There's going to be a famine," he said. "At first, all will seem fine. Lots of food will grow for seven years, but then hardly any food will grow for seven years after that. If you don't want your people to starve, you need someone to help get the country ready."

"Joseph, the job is yours!" said Pharaoh, and he gave Joseph a gold chain and a special chariot. Joseph became a great leader. He made all the farmers in Egypt store up lots of grain, so that when the famine came everyone still had enough to eat.

Soon the famine spread to the land of Canaan, and Joseph's brothers decided to go to Egypt to buy grain. When they saw Joseph they didn't know it was him. They thought he was a great Egyptian leader, and they all bowed down to him. It happened just as Joseph had dreamed. When Joseph told his brothers who he was, they were afraid. But Joseph forgave them. "You wanted to hurt me," he said, "but God had a plan. It was God who brought me here, to save the lives of many people."

# The Baby in the Reeds

Where's this
in the Bible?

Exodus 1–2

Jacob and his family decided to move to Egypt. They lived there for many years and had lots of children. When those children grew up, they had lots of children too, until there were thousands of Jacob's descendants living in the land of Egypt. They were known as the Israelites, after the name that the angel had given Jacob on his journey back to Canaan.

The years went by and a new pharaoh, who had not known Joseph, ruled over Egypt. He was worried about how strong the Israelites were becoming, and how many there were of them. So he decided to make them work as his slaves. But that made no difference. The Israelites remained strong and kept having more children. Then the pharaoh came up with a terrible plan. He called his soldiers together. "There are too many of these Israelites," he said. "Go and kill all their baby boys!"

But there was one Israelite woman who had a plan of her own. She took her little baby and gently wrapped him in a blanket. Then, early in the morning, she put him in a basket and hid him in the reeds at the edge of the River Nile. The baby's older sister, Miriam, waited nearby to see what would happen.

An Egyptian princess came down to the river to bathe. She noticed the basket among the reeds and sent her slave-girl to fetch it. When she opened the basket, there was the baby! Straight away Miriam ran up to the princess. She bowed her head and said, "If you like, I could ask one of the Israelite women to nurse him for you." The princess agreed, and Miriam took the baby back to his own mother.

When her son had grown big enough, his mother took him to the princess, who adopted him as her own child. She called him Moses which means "saved from the water".

# God Calls Moses

Where's this in the Bible?

Exodus 2–3

Moses grew up to be an Egyptian prince. But when he saw how the Egyptians had forced the Israelites to be their slaves, he was angry. One day, he saw an Egyptian beating an Israelite slave. Moses tried to stop him. There was a struggle, and he killed the Egyptian. Moses realized he had made a bad mistake. What could he do? If he was found out, Pharaoh would kill him! Quickly, Moses buried the Egyptian's body in the sand and then he ran away into the desert.

For many years, Moses lived in the desert looking after sheep. But then, one day, something happened that would change his life, and the life of all the Israelites, forever. Moses was leading his sheep along a mountain path when he looked up and in the distance he saw a bush that seemed to be on fire. As he moved closer, he saw that the bush was full of flames, and yet it wasn't burning up!

Then, out of the bush, he heard the voice of God say: "I am the God of Abraham, Isaac, and Jacob. I have seen the suffering of my people in Egypt, and I have come to rescue them from their slavery. I am sending you to tell Pharaoh that he must let my people go."

Moses was so shocked that at first he couldn't speak. But after a while he found the courage to ask a question. "If I go to the people of Israel," he said, "and tell them, 'God has sent me,' they will ask me, 'What is his name?' Then what should I tell them?"

God replied, "Tell them 'Yahweh', the God of Abraham, Isaac, and Jacob, has sent you. That is my name forever." Moses was afraid, but God promised to be with him. He sent Aaron, Moses' brother, to help him.

What else in God's big story links up with this?

**Isaiah's Vision of Yahweh**
p. 104

# Let My People Go!

Where's this in the Bible?

Exodus 7–12

God had decided to rescue the Israelites from their slavery in Egypt. He sent Moses and Aaron to Pharaoh, and Moses said to Pharaoh, "Yahweh, the God of the Israelites, has sent me to tell you to let his people go!" But Pharaoh wouldn't listen. So God told Moses to warn Pharaoh that bad things were going to happen if Pharaoh didn't do what Moses said.

First, the water in the River Nile turned into blood. But Pharaoh wouldn't let the Israelites go.

Second, God sent a plague of frogs. They jumped all over people's houses and hopped into their cooking pots. They were everywhere! But still Pharaoh wouldn't let the Israelites go.

Third, God sent a plague of gnats. They crawled over everything and made everyone itch. Pharaoh's own magicians told him, "This is the finger of God." But still Pharaoh wouldn't let the Israelites go.

Fourth, God sent flies, swarming and buzzing everywhere.
Fifth, all the Egyptians' animals died: horses, donkeys, camels, cows, and sheep.
Sixth, God sent boils on the Egyptians, making their skin bubble up and itch.
But still Pharaoh wouldn't listen.

Seventh, God sent a thunderstorm and heavy hail.
Eighth, God sent locusts, which ate up all the crops.
Ninth, God sent darkness over the whole land.
Pharaoh pretended he would let the Israelites go, but then he didn't.

What would it take to make Pharaoh listen and let God's people go?

THE OLD TESTAMENT

# The First Passover

Where's this in the Bible?

Exodus 12

This is how God rescued his people. God told Moses to tell everyone to prepare a special meal made of roast lamb, flatbread, and herbs. Each Israelite family had to smear some of the lamb's blood on their doorposts. Then, when everyone was asleep, God would send the angel of death through the land. If the angel saw a doorpost with blood on it, the angel would pass over the house, and everyone inside would be safe.

That night the angel of death came to Egypt. In every Egyptian home, the firstborn son died. But the Israelites were safe.

After that, the Egyptians couldn't wait for the Israelites to leave. "Out of my sight!" shouted Pharaoh. "We don't want you here anymore!"

The Israelites didn't need to be told twice. Quickly they packed up all their belongings, along with all their animals, and got ready to leave the land of Egypt.

But before the people left, God told them to remember the special meal they had eaten. They called the special meal "Passover". God told them to eat it together once a year. It would remind them of the night when the angel passed over their houses and Yahweh, their God, rescued them from Egypt.

THE OLD TESTAMENT

What else in God's big story links up with this?

**Jesus' Last Meal with His Disciples**
p. 204

# A Journey through the Sea

Where's this in the Bible?

Exodus 13–15

At last, they had escaped! The Israelites were so happy to leave behind their lives of slavery. Thousands of them closed their doors for the last time and set out together. In the daytime, God led the way in a large cloud, and at night-time he went ahead of them in a huge column of fire. They travelled for several days until they reached a big stretch of water called the Red Sea, where they started to make camp.

But then they heard a noise. A distant rumbling sound was coming from behind them. They turned to see what it could be, and there, racing toward them with horses and chariots, was the Egyptian army. Pharaoh had changed his mind again!

With the sea in front of them and the Egyptians behind them, the Israelites were trapped. They were very frightened, but God told Moses to tell the people to trust in him and he would save them. Then Moses climbed onto a high rock and stretched his arm out over the sea. As Moses did that, a strong wind began to blow across the water. It blew and blew until at last it had cleared a pathway through the middle of the sea. Then Moses told the Israelites to gather up their belongings and walk across. There were two enormous walls of water towering above them! It was amazing and very scary, but they kept going until they were safe on the other side.

As the Israelites were making their way across, the Egyptians were getting closer and closer. Then, when the Egyptians reached the edge of the sea, they tried to cross as well. But when they were about half-way across, the wind suddenly stopped, and the walls of water crashed back down and drowned the whole army. The Israelites camped on the other side of the sea, and Moses' sister Miriam led all the women in a victory song, thanking and praising God for saving his people.

What else in God's big story links up with this?

**Joshua Takes the Lead**
p. 60

**Jesus is Baptized**
p. 148

# Water from a Rock

Where's this in the Bible?

Exodus 16–17

The Israelites set off walking through the desert. They walked for miles and miles during the day, and at night they stopped to set up their tents and make camp.

If they thought life was going to be easy after leaving Egypt, they were wrong. What were they going to eat? What were they going to drink? What about all their animals? They were hungry and thirsty too.

The people grumbled at Moses and Aaron. "Why did you bring us out of Egypt?" they moaned. "At least we had plenty to eat there."

So God gave them food. Every evening a flock of quails would fly across the sky and land in the camp, providing the people with fresh meat to eat. And every morning, once the early dew had gone, there was something strange and white all over the ground. It looked like bread and tasted like wafers made with honey. The people didn't know what it was, so they called it "manna", which means, "What is it?"

But the people were still thirsty. They became very angry. Moses asked God, "What should I do with these people? They're almost ready to kill me!" God told him to climb onto a rock and hit it with a big stick. Moses did what God said, and a flood of water gushed out of the rock.

There was enough water for everyone to drink, and the animals too.

What else in God's big story links up with this?

**The Woman at the Well**
p. 168

**Jesus Feeds a Big Crowd**
p. 170

THE OLD TESTAMENT

# On God's Mountain

Where's this in the Bible?

Exodus 19, 20

The Israelites' journey through the desert had brought them near to a large mountain. It was called Mount Sinai. But it was no ordinary mountain. As they approached, the people saw that the top of the mountain was on fire, with thick dark clouds swirling around it. Then, as they got closer, they heard loud claps of thunder coming from the clouds, and flashes of lightning pierced the sky. The people were terrified, and all the children covered their ears when they heard the thunder!

God told Moses to climb up the mountain and meet him there. God had decided to tell Moses about his plan to come and live with his people. God was going to make a special agreement with them. If they kept to the agreement they would be like kings and priests, looking after God's creation and leading the whole world in worship. The people watched in amazement as Moses went up the mountain. Higher and higher he climbed, until he disappeared into the dark clouds. Then, in a great voice, God told the people how they must live. He gave them these ten important rules:

"I am Yahweh. You may worship no other gods but me.
Don't make any pictures or statues for worship.
Don't use my name for wrong purposes.
Remember to rest from work on the seventh day of the week.
Respect your father and your mother.
Don't murder.
Don't be unfaithful in marriage.
Don't steal.
Don't tell lies about people.
Don't keep longing for things that aren't yours."

What else in God's big story links up with this?

**Jesus Teaches People about God**
p. 162

THE OLD TESTAMENT

# Aaron Makes an Idol

Where's this in the Bible?

Exodus 32

Moses came back down the mountain and built an altar to God. The people gathered round, and he told them about God's special agreement. Then God called Moses to go up the mountain again. God gave Moses two tablets of stone, on which were written the ten important rules that made up the special agreement. God wanted the people to always remember them, so that they would be his people and he, Yahweh, would be their God.

But first, God wanted to explain to Moses lots more about how he planned to live with his people. Moses was on the mountain for a long time, and the people below started to think he would never come back. "We don't know what's happened to him!" they grumbled. "He's led us out here to the desert and now he's gone off and left us on our own." Aaron tried to calm them down, but the people just kept on grumbling. Then some of them began to doubt God. They told Aaron to make an idol for them to worship instead of Yahweh.

Aaron was afraid of the people, so he did what they wanted. He helped them to make an idol. It was a statue of a young bull-calf, made of gold. When the people saw the calf, they became very excited and started shouting and dancing around it. But then, to their surprise, Moses came back! At once the dancing stopped, and everyone looked at Moses, who was holding the two stone tablets that God had given him. Then Moses saw the idol, and his face grew red with anger. He was so angry that he lifted the stone tablets high above his head and CRASH! He smashed them to pieces on the ground.

God was angry with the people too. But Moses asked God to give them another chance. In the end God decided he would still be with them. He gave Moses two new stone tablets and wrote on them the ten important rules that made up the special agreement between Yahweh and his people.

What else in God's big story links up with this?

**The Kingdom is Broken in Two**
p. 96

# God's Beautiful Tent

Where's this in the Bible?

Exodus 35–38, 40

When Moses was on the mountain, God told him, "I need a special place where I can live with my people." It would be a huge, beautiful tent and inside there would be special furniture. The tent and its furniture would be looked after by priests. The task of the priests was to serve God and lead the rest of the people in worshipping God properly. Aaron, Moses' brother, would be their leader. They called him the "high priest".

Moses told the people to bring lots of beautiful things: jewels, leather, fine linen, gold, silver, and bronze. He gave everything to two wise craftsmen, Bezalel and Oholiab, who were in charge of making the tent. Everything had to be perfectly crafted, like a mirror of heaven.

Bezalel made a big wooden chest, covered in pure gold. On top of the chest he carved two golden angels, one on each side. Inside the chest they would keep the stone tablets that recorded the special agreement, based on the ten important rules. They called the chest God's Ark. Next, Bezalel made a special table, also covered in gold. This was where the priests would place fresh bread as a sign that God was present and would provide for all the people. Then Bezalel made a magnificent seven-branched lampstand, and the altars where the priests would offer worship.

At last, everything was ready. Until now, God had stayed hidden in a great shining cloud high up on the mountain. But now, something wonderful began to happen. All the people watched the great cloud as it slowly floated down from the mountain toward them. At first they were puzzled and afraid, but then the cloud stopped outside the special tent. They watched in amazement as the cloud filled the tent with God's shining glory. They knew that Yahweh, the one true God, had come to live with them. Moses went in to speak with God. When he came out his face was shining.

What else in God's big story links up with this?

**The Wonderful Temple**
p. 92

**Jesus, the New Beginning**
p. 282

# Sin and Forgiveness

Where's this in the Bible?

Leviticus 16

God is living and glorious. He didn't just make things to be alive. God is life itself. But humans grow old, become ill, and die. Even worse, humans do and say bad things that spoil life, leading them away from God and toward death. We call this "sin".

Sin is like a thick fog that stops people from seeing how to live good lives that are pleasing to God. The more people do bad things, the thicker the fog becomes. And the thicker the fog becomes, the harder it is for people to see the path that leads to God.

God wanted to show his people how to break through the fog of sin. Only then could he be with them and show them the way to light and life.

So God told the people to bring him some of their animals. The animals' blood was a sign of life. When the animals were killed, their life-blood would wash away the traces of sin and death. At the same time, the people would say sorry to God. All this meant that God could stay with them and forgive them, despite all the wrong things they did.

Once a year, this had to be done in a special way. God's special tent would be thoroughly cleaned, and Aaron, the high priest, would choose a goat and bring it to God's tent in front of all the people. Aaron would put his hands on the goat's head and say sorry to God for the people's sins. Then a man would send the goat away into the desert. This was to show that the people's sins were being taken away.

It showed that the people were forgiven, and that Yahweh their God would stay with them.

What else in God's big story links up with this?

**The Suffering Servant**
p. 120

**Jesus is Crucified**
p. 216

THE OLD TESTAMENT

# Jubilee!

Where's this in the Bible?

Leviticus 25

God wanted his people to remember how he had rescued them from Egypt. He also wanted them to look forward to the day when they would enter the Promised Land, the land God had promised to Abraham and his children. And now they were nearly there! To help the people remember, God gave them special days, called holy days. On these holy days the people would stop working, and instead they would spend time together and thank God for everything he had done for them.

Once a week, on the seventh day, the people were to stop work and rest completely. This day was called the "Sabbath", which means "to rest". It would remind them that one day they would rest in the land that God had promised.

Once a year, they were to celebrate the festival of Passover. They would eat flatbread, like the people had done on the day God rescued them from Egypt.

They would also celebrate the beginning of the harvest, and seven weeks later they would celebrate the full harvest. This was called the festival of "Pentecost", when they would remember the time when God gave Moses his special agreement on Mount Sinai.

When they arrived in the Promised Land, they would farm the land for six years. Then, every seventh year, they would stop ploughing and planting and allow the land to rest. After every 49 years (7 x 7), they would have an extra-special celebration. This was called the "Jubilee". The priests would blow the Jubilee horns. Everybody who owed anything to anyone would have their debts cancelled. Every family, even slaves, would be able to return to their own house.

The whole land belonged to Yahweh. He wanted everyone to share it fairly.

What else in God's big story links up with this?

**What is the Sabbath For?**
p. 160

**Jesus Sends God's Holy Spirit**
p. 230

# The People Grumble Again

Where's this in the Bible?

Numbers 13, 21

The Israelites were getting closer to the Promised Land. Moses decided to send 12 men ahead of them. Their job was to spy out the land and find out what they could about the people who lived there. The 12 spies were gone a long time, and when they came back two of them were carrying a huge bunch of grapes. The grapes were so big and heavy that the two men had to hang them from a long pole that they carried between them!

Two of the spies told everyone what a wonderful, fertile land they had seen, with lots of good places where they could build their houses and farms. But ten of the spies didn't agree. "We can't possibly live in this land," they said. "We saw giants there, and cities with enormous walls to keep us out."

Two of the spies, Joshua and Caleb, believed God's promise. "God is with us," they said. But the others wanted to choose a new leader instead of Moses. They were afraid to go on and wanted to go back to Egypt.

God was disappointed with those people for not believing his promise. He told them that one day his glory would surely fill the whole world.

Because the people didn't believe, God made them wander in the desert for many more years. But the people just went on grumbling. So God sent poisonous snakes into the camp, and they bit the people who grumbled. After that, the people said they were sorry. Then God told Moses to make a snake out of copper and put it on a pole where everyone could see it. Anyone who had been bitten by a real snake had to look at the copper snake on the pole, and they would be healed.

What else in God's big story links up with this?

**Jesus is Crucified**
p. 216

THE OLD TESTAMENT

54

# Balaam and the Talking Donkey

Where's this in the Bible?

Numbers 22

The Israelites continued their long journey through the desert until they reached a country called Moab. The king of Moab was afraid when he heard the Israelites were near. He wanted to stop them from getting any closer. "I know!" he said. "I'll send a prophet to curse them." (A prophet is someone who hears messages from God. God gives the prophet a message and then they pass it on to everyone who will listen.)

The king sent a message to a prophet called Balaam. "I'm going to find the Israelites," said the king, "and when I find them I will send for you. You must come and curse them, and that will make them go away." Balaam didn't like the sound of this, but he got on his donkey and went to find the king. He hadn't gone far when suddenly the donkey turned off the pathway into a field. God had sent an angel with a sword to stand in the way, but only the donkey could see it. Balaam hit the donkey with a stick and made it go back. Then the angel stood in front of the donkey again and blocked the way completely. The donkey sat down, and Balaam hit it again.

Then God made the donkey speak. "I'm your donkey!" it said. "Why are you hitting me? I've never disobeyed you before." Balaam couldn't believe his ears. He thought he must be going mad! Then God allowed Balaam to see the angel for himself, and he realized that God didn't want him to curse the Israelites.

At last Balaam found the place where the king was waiting, but instead of cursing the Israelites, Balaam blessed them. He spoke about a future king who would rise like a star and defeat Israel's enemies. The king of Moab was furious. He had made a big mistake. He thought he could tell Balaam what to do. But a real prophet only takes instructions from God, not from a mere man, even if he is a king.

# Promises and Warnings

Where's this in the Bible?

Deuteronomy 28

It was almost time for the Israelites to enter the Promised Land. To make sure they were ready, Moses explained again what God's special agreement would mean.

This is what he said:

"Remember how Yahweh your God rescued you from Egypt! Remember all he has done for you, and show your love and thanks by worshipping him with all your heart. Serve him all the time, and obey all his rules.

"If you do this, the land will be fruitful. You will have plenty to eat. Your sheep and cattle will be well fed and happy. All the other nations in the world will see that God has blessed you.

"But if you disobey, and worship idols, then the land will stop producing good food. Your animals will suffer. Enemies will come and attack you. Finally, you will be attacked by a foreign army and forced to live in exile in a strange place, far away from the Promised Land. Instead of being blessed you will be cursed.

"But if that happens, and afterwards you turn back to Yahweh with all your heart, he will forgive you and bring you back from exile, back to the Land of Promise."

In this way, Moses urged the people to choose life rather than death, to be blessed rather than cursed.

What else in God's big story links up with this?

**Exile!**
p. 112

**Jesus Goes into the Desert**
p. 150

# Joshua Takes the Lead

Where's this
in the Bible?

Joshua 3–4

The Israelites were camped near the River Jordan. It was deep, and flowing fast. They could see across the river into the land that God had promised to give them.

By this time, Moses had died and now Joshua was the leader. (He was one of the two spies who had believed God's promises.) God told Joshua to be strong, to have courage, and be careful to keep all his rules.

On the other side of the river was the city of Jericho. Joshua sent two men across the river to spy on the city. The king of Jericho found out and sent his soldiers to arrest them. But a brave woman called Rahab helped them by hiding them on the roof of her house. The house was built into the wall that went around the city. When it was dark, Rahab lowered a long rope through a window and the two spies climbed down the wall and escaped. They came back to the camp and found Joshua. They told him the people of Jericho were afraid because they knew that the God of Israel was powerful and had rescued them from Egypt.

The next day, Joshua told the priests to pick up the Ark (the big chest containing the special agreement) and carry it into the middle of the River Jordan. When the priests stepped into the river, the water stopped flowing, making a clear pathway over to the other side. The priests stood in the middle, and all the Israelites crossed over safely.

Then Joshua chose 12 men. He told each of them to take a stone from the place where the priests had stood. They made a pile of all the stones on the riverbank and made a tower. It was to remind everyone how Yahweh their God had brought them into the Promised Land.

What else in God's big story links up with this?

**A Journey through
the Sea**
p. 40

# The Capture of Jericho

Where's this in the Bible?

Joshua 5–7

After they had crossed the River Jordan, the Israelites marched toward the city of Jericho. Suddenly, Joshua saw a man with a sword. "Are you on our side," demanded Joshua, "or with our enemies?"

"I am the commander of Yahweh's army," the man replied. At this, Joshua fell at the man's feet and said, "I am at your command. What should I do?"

The commander of the Lord's army replied, "Take off your sandals, for you are standing on holy ground."

God told Joshua what to do, and the people obeyed. They marched round the city of Jericho every day for a week. Seven priests led the way, blowing on seven trumpets made from rams' horns. On the seventh day they marched round the city seven times. The people had to be absolutely quiet until Joshua gave the command. Then, after the seventh time of marching around, Joshua told everyone to SHOUT!

They all shouted at the tops of their voices, and then something amazing happened. The city walls fell down flat! The Israelites charged in and captured the city. There was a lot of fighting, but the Israelites made sure they rescued Rahab, the brave woman who had helped the spies.

The Israelites burned everything in the city, except for some precious things that they put in God's special tent. But one man stole some of the precious things for himself. God was angry about that, so the next time the Israelites tried to capture a city, they couldn't do it until the man owned up and was punished.

# Gideon the Brave

Where's this in the Bible?

Judges 6–8

The Israelites had to fight many more battles before they could live peacefully in the Promised Land. They just wanted to settle down, look after their families, and be free to worship Yahweh, the one true God who had rescued them from Egypt. But other nations kept attacking them and tried to make them worship idols.

Once, the Israelites were attacked by the Midianites, who made them worship an idol called "Baal". When that happened, God chose a man called Gideon to put things right. "The Midianites have built an altar for Baal," said God. "You must break it down and build an altar for me instead." Gideon did as God commanded, but still the Midianites kept attacking.

Gideon decided to look for men who would help him fight the Midianites. But first, he asked for a sign that God would be with them. That night, Gideon put a fleece outside on the ground and prayed that in the morning there would be dew on the fleece but not on the ground. And that is just what happened. The next night, he put the fleece outside again, but this time he prayed that the dew would be on the ground and not on the fleece. In the morning Gideon found the fleece, and it was completely dry! Then he knew God would be with him.

Gideon gathered a large army, but God told him he would need only a little one. So Gideon chose a small group of men and went to look for the Midianites. By now it was night, and Gideon's soldiers each carried a torch of fire hidden inside a jar. Each man also carried a trumpet. The soldiers climbed a hill and saw the enemy's camp in the valley below. Gideon gave the signal. The soldiers blew the trumpets and smashed the jars on the ground. CRASH! The Midianites jumped up in alarm and ran out of their tents. They leaped onto their camels and tried to get away. But Gideon and his men chased after them and won a great victory.

# Samson the Strong

Where's this in the Bible?

Judges 13–16

The Israelites enjoyed peace for a few years, but soon other nations started to attack them. This time it was the Philistines. God chose a man called Samson to rescue his people. Samson was incredibly strong. He was so strong that once he killed a fierce lion with his bare hands. Later on, some bees made a nest inside the lion's dead body. Samson noticed the bees had made some honey, which made him think of a riddle: "Out of the eater came something to eat. Out of the strong came something sweet." Samson told the riddle to the Philistines. They tried their hardest, but none of them could guess what it meant. It made them very annoyed!

The Philistines were afraid of Samson, so they got some of Samson's own people to tie him up. But Samson burst out of the ropes and easily escaped. Later, the Philistines persuaded Samson's girlfriend, Delilah, to find out what made him so strong. Delilah asked him so many times that finally Samson told her. "The secret of my strength," he said, "is that my hair has never been cut. It is a sign that I belong to God." So, one night, when Samson was asleep, Delilah got someone to cut off all his hair. When Samson awoke, his strength had gone, and the Philistines seized him and put him in prison.

Later that year, the Philistines held a big party. They put Samson in chains and led him in, intending to make fun of him. But while he was in prison Samson's hair had begun to grow back, and now he was feeling stronger. All the Philistines were laughing at him. But Samson moved toward the huge pillars that held up the roof. He stood there for a while and quietly prayed, "Oh Yahweh, give me strength for one last time." Then he put his hands on the pillars and pushed against them. Harder and harder he pushed, until the pillars cracked and crumbled, and then, CRASH! The roof caved in and the whole building collapsed. Samson was killed, and so were all the Philistines.

# A Husband for Ruth

Where's this in the Bible?

Ruth 1–4

Around that time, there was a girl called Ruth who lived in Moab, not far from the land of Israel. When she grew up, Ruth married an Israelite man whose father and mother had moved to Moab from Israel. But then Ruth's husband died, and she became a widow. Sadly, Ruth's mother-in-law, Naomi, had also lost her husband. Ruth loved Naomi, and she also had faith in Yahweh, Israel's God. So when Naomi told Ruth she was going back to live in the land of Israel, Ruth begged to go with her.

It was harvest-time when they came to the little town of Bethlehem. Naomi told Ruth to follow behind the men working in the fields and to pick up some of the grain they had left. The field Ruth chose belonged to Naomi's cousin, Boaz. He welcomed Ruth. He was pleased that she wanted to live in Israel and worship Yahweh.

Naomi told Ruth to let Boaz know that they were cousins. So, one night, Ruth crept into the harvest store, where Boaz had fallen asleep, and lay down beside him. He woke up and was startled to find her there. But he promised her it would all work out fine. He gave her plenty of grain to take home to Naomi.

The next day, Boaz announced to the people of Bethlehem that he was going to buy his cousin's family property, and that he and Ruth would be married.

Later, Boaz and Ruth had a baby. They called him Obed. When Obed grew up, he had a son called Jesse. When Jesse grew up, he had a son called David. And when David grew up, he became a great king.

# Hannah's Special Child

Where's this in the Bible?

1 Samuel 1–3

Many years had passed since the Israelites had left Egypt and entered the Promised Land. Some of them still worshipped God at the beautiful tent that their ancestors had brought with them from the desert. One year, a young woman called Hannah decided to make a journey to the special tent. Hannah was married, but she had no children, which made her very sad. When she arrived at God's tent, she prayed, "Dear God, if you will only give me a son, I will give him back to you, to serve you here forever."

The next year, Hannah gave birth to a son. She called him "Samuel", which means "asked from God". When Samuel was old enough, Hannah took him to see God's beautiful tent. She was going to fulfil her promise to give her son back to God. She gave the little boy to the priests who looked after God's tent. They would now take care of him and teach him to serve God. Hannah visited Samuel every year, and as he grew bigger she would bring him new clothes that she had made for him.

One night, God called, "Samuel, Samuel!" Samuel thought it was Eli the priest, but Eli said, "It wasn't me. Go back to bed."

Then God called again. "Samuel, Samuel!" Samuel went to Eli again, but again the priest said it wasn't him. When it happened a third time, Eli realized it was God calling, and he told Samuel that next time he should say, "Speak, Lord, your servant is listening."

God called again, so Samuel replied, "Speak, Lord, your servant is listening."

God gave Samuel a message for Eli and his family. And so Samuel began to be a prophet while he was still a boy.

What else in God's big story links up with this?

**Zechariah and the Angel**
p. 138

# Where is the Ark?

Where's this
in the Bible?

1 Samuel 4–6

The Philistines were attacking Israel again. The Israelites wanted God to fight for them, so they went into God's tent and took out the Ark (the golden chest containing the stone tablets setting out God's special agreement). Then they carried the Ark onto the battlefield. But the Philistines won the battle and stole the Ark.

"Ha!" shouted the Philistines. "Look what we've got!" They thought the Ark was a fine trophy. They carried it back from the battle and put it in their temple, where they kept a statue of their god, Dagon. But that night, something strange happened. The statue of Dagon fell over, PLONK, flat on its face! When the Philistines saw their god lying on the floor in front of the Ark, they were frightened and worried. How could that have happened?

They placed Dagon on his feet again next to the Ark and made sure the doors to the temple were locked. But by the next morning, Dagon had fallen over, PLONK, just like before. And this time his head and hands were broken off. Now the Philistines were really worried.

They were wondering what to do when some of them began to feel very ill. "What's happening to us?" they cried. Then someone pointed out that all this trouble had started when they had stolen the Ark. "Let's get rid of it!" they said. So the Philistines grabbed the Ark and put it on a cart. Then they got two cows to pull the cart away and they watched to see where they would take it. The cows knew just where to go. They carried the Ark straight back to the land of Israel.

By this time, Samuel was a grown man, and everyone knew he was God's prophet. He told the people that if they were going to welcome the Ark back, and with it God's special agreement, they would all have to promise to worship Yahweh, the only true God.

# Who Should Be King?

Where's this in the Bible?

1 Samuel 8–16

The people of Israel were now settled in the Promised Land, and they decided they wanted a king to rule over them like the kings of all the other nations around them. Samuel warned the people that kings often behaved badly. Some only cared about themselves instead of caring for their subjects. But the people were sure they needed a king, so after praying to God, Samuel announced that God had chosen a man called Saul. Samuel poured some holy oil on Saul's head, and prayed that God's Spirit would help Saul to be a good ruler.

Saul led the people in battle against their enemies. At first he did well, but later he decided he didn't want to do all the things God told him to do. In the end, Samuel told Saul that God had rejected him. Soon, he would no longer be king.

Around that time, God said to Samuel, "You must go to Bethlehem. There you will find a man named Jesse. I have chosen one of his sons to be king instead of Saul."

Jesse brought seven of his sons to see Samuel, but none of them was the one God had chosen. "Are these all the sons you have?" asked Samuel. "Well," said Jesse, "I suppose there's David, my youngest. But he's not here. He's out in the fields looking after the sheep."

"Fetch him at once!" Samuel ordered. And they all waited, and waited, and waited, while someone went off to look for him. When at last David was found, God said to Samuel, "This is the one. Anoint him." So Samuel anointed David with holy oil in front of his brothers. God's Spirit came powerfully upon David from that moment onwards. But it wasn't yet time for him to be king, and David went back to his sheep.

What else in God's big story links up with this?

**Who Do You Think I Am?**
p. 174

# David the Giant Killer

Where's this in the Bible?

1 Samuel 17–18

Around that time, another battle between Israel and the Philistines was looming. Some of David's brothers were in the army, and David's father had told him to take them some food. As he got near, David heard shouting, and when he saw his brothers he asked what was going on. "It's the giant," they said. "He's huge! He's called Goliath, and he's the Philistines' champion. Every day he comes out and challenges us to send one of our men to fight him. But nobody dares."

David went to King Saul. "This Philistine has insulted God's people," he said. "I will kill him just like I killed the lions and bears when they attacked my sheep." Saul wanted to lend David his armour, but it was too big and heavy. And so, armed only with his shepherd's sling, David went out to meet the giant. On the way, he stopped by a stream and picked up five smooth stones.

When Goliath saw David, he was furious. "Come any nearer and I'll feed your body to the birds!" roared Goliath. David replied, "You come to me with sword and spear, but I come to you in the name of Yahweh, the living God!" Then David took a stone, placed it carefully in his sling, and hurled it at Goliath. The sharp stone hit him hard on the forehead, and he fell to the ground in a heap. Then, before the giant could get up, David ran over, grabbed Goliath's own sword, and cut off his head.

When the Philistines saw that their champion was dead, they turned tail and ran away. And when the Israelites saw the Philistines fleeing the battle, they gave a loud cheer and chased after them.

King Saul was impressed with David's skill and courage. He brought David into his household, and David became close friends with Saul's son, Jonathan.

# Yahweh is My Shepherd

Where's this
in the Bible?

Psalm 23

*When David was a boy, he used to make up songs while he was looking*
*after the sheep. This one gives thanks for God's care and guidance.*

Yahweh is my shepherd
There is nothing more I need!
He takes me to the green, green fields
To rest awhile and feed.

He lets me drink from cool, clear streams,
Making me feel like new;
He leads me on the proper path,
Since to his name he's true.

Yes, even if we have to go
Through a dark and deadly way,
I'll never be afraid, because
He's with me every day.

I see his stick and staff and know
He'll keep me safe from danger.
He lays the table for a feast
In sight of foe or stranger.

He pours fresh oil upon my head.
My cup is filled to the top;
His goodness and his mercy
Follow me, and never stop.

So evermore in Yahweh's house
I now will make my home:
And there I'll dwell in perfect safety
Through all the years to come.

What else in God's big story
links up with this?

**The Good Shepherd**
p. 188

# David Goes on the Run

Where's this in the Bible?

1 Samuel 16, 26, 31; 2 Samuel 1

After Saul became king, he would sometimes become depressed and angry. Saul's servants heard that David was a gifted harp player, and they thought it would be good if David could come and play some soothing music for the king. So David was brought to the palace to play the harp, and when Saul heard the music he began to feel better.

But after David had killed Goliath, Saul became bitter and envious. He worried that David was becoming more famous than he was. That made Saul even angrier than before, and he tried to kill David. Jonathan, Saul's son, tried to stop his father, but then Saul became angry with Jonathan, too.

In the end, David had to run away. Saul and his men tried to hunt him down, but David hid with some friends in a cave, and then moved around from place to place so that Saul couldn't find him. Once, David and his friends found Saul asleep in his camp. David's friends wanted to kill Saul, but David wouldn't let them. "He's still God's anointed king," he said.

Saul never did manage to capture David. Later, both Saul and Jonathan were killed in another battle with the Philistines. When David heard of this, he broke down and wept. Jonathan was the closest friend David had ever had.

# God's Promise to David

Where's this in the Bible?

2 Samuel 5, 7–8

Israel's king and the king's son were both dead, and for a time there was a struggle between the men who served Saul and the followers of David. In the end David and his followers won, and David was crowned king.

When David became king, he built himself a big palace in Jerusalem, his capital city. Then he thought he would build a house for God. The Ark, containing God's special agreement was still kept in God's special tent, and David wanted to give it a better home.

Nathan the prophet came to see David with a message. "This is what God told me," he said.

"All this time I have lived in a tent. And I have taken you, a shepherd boy, and made you the king. You will make my people safe. I know you want to build me a house, but instead I am going to make a 'house' for you. After you have died, I promise to raise up your son to be the king. He is the one who will build the house where I will live. And his descendants, the 'house' of David, will be kings forever."

David was amazed and very grateful. He prayed and thanked God for making such a wonderful promise.

What else in God's big story links up with this?

**The Wonderful Temple**
p. 92

**Mary Has a Special Visitor**
p. 140

# David's Terrible Sin

In those days, when Israel was at war with its enemies, King David himself would often lead his army into battle. But one day he left that to his army commander and stayed behind in Jerusalem. That evening, David went up onto the flat roof of his palace, and as he looked down on the houses below he saw a woman bathing. She was Bathsheba, the wife of Uriah, one of the soldiers who was fighting in the army.

Bathsheba was beautiful. David couldn't stop thinking about her. So he sent some servants to bring Bathsheba to the palace. He slept with her, and afterwards he sent her back home. Some weeks later Bathsheba discovered she was going to have a baby. She sent a message to tell David that the baby was his. When he heard that, David ordered Bathsheba's husband back from the battle and tried to persuade him to go and see his wife. But Uriah refused to go home when other soldiers were still fighting. So David told the army commander to send Uriah back to the battle and put him in the front row of the fighting. That would surely mean Uriah would be killed. And that's what happened. Uriah died in battle, which meant that David could now take Bathsheba to be his wife.

Nathan the prophet came to see David. He told him a story about a rich man who had lots of sheep, but the rich man was greedy and stole a pet lamb that belonged to a poor man who lived nearby. It was the only lamb the poor man had. David was furious with the rich man. "Who is he?" he asked. "Whoever he is, he deserves to die."

"You are the man!" said Nathan. "You have stolen Uriah's wife. And you have killed him." Then David realized what a terrible sin he had committed.

# Rebellion!

Where's this in the Bible?

2 Samuel 15–18

King David had several wives and lots of children. One of his sons, Absalom, grew up to be a proud and vain young man, with long flowing hair. He thought he would make a much better king than his father. He made friends with some powerful people and sent messengers throughout the land to stir up rebellion.

Absalom lied to his father, pretending to be loyal while secretly plotting against him. More and more people joined the conspiracy and soon Absalom had assembled an army. Then he decided to act. He sent a messenger to Jerusalem, informing David that he, Absalom, was now the king.

At this, David quickly gathered some of his loyal followers. He left Jerusalem and led them across the River Jordan to safety.

Absalom gathered his army and went into battle against the men in David's army. David told his men not to harm Absalom. But it was not to be. The battle raged all day, and Absalom's men were losing. Absalom decided he had to get away, but the mule he was riding ran under a tree and Absalom's long hair got caught in the branches. He couldn't move! He was hanging there, helpless, when some of David's men found him and killed him.

The commander of the army sent messengers to tell David that the battle was won and that Absalom was dead. The messengers thought David would be so pleased to hear the news. But they were wrong. David went up to his room and wept. "Oh Absalom, my son, my son!" he cried. "If only I could have died instead of you."

# The Wisest Man on Earth

Where's this in the Bible?

1 Kings 2–3

David reigned over Israel for a long time. When he died, his son Solomon became king. Solomon was still quite a young man. He loved Yahweh, the one true God, and worshipped him only. One night, in a dream, God spoke to him. "Ask what you want me to give you," God said.

Solomon knew it was hard to be a good king, so he asked God for wisdom. He wanted to understand his people and make good decisions. God was pleased. He gave Solomon so much wisdom that he became the wisest man on earth.

One day, two women were brought into Solomon's palace. They were shouting and screaming at each other. Solomon called for silence and asked what had happened. One of the king's servants explained that both women had recently had babies, but during the night one of the babies had died. Now, both women were claiming that the living child was theirs. Solomon ordered one of his guards to bring a sword. "Cut the baby in two," he said. "They can have half each."

"Go ahead," said one of the women, who suddenly didn't seem to care. Then Solomon turned to the other woman. "No, no, my lord!" she cried. "Whatever you do, please don't do that! Let her have the baby." And at once Solomon knew that she was the true mother, since she would do anything to save her child from being killed.

After that, everyone was impressed with Solomon's wisdom, and all the people knew that God was with him.

# Wisdom for Life

Where's this in the Bible?

Proverbs;
Ecclesiastes

*King Solomon was famous for the many proverbs and wise sayings he invented. Here are just a few well-known examples. They remain true nearly 3,000 years after he lived!*

A gentle word is a tree of life,
but a deceitful tongue crushes the spirit.
Proverbs 15:4

Like apples of gold in a silver dish
are the right words spoken at the right time.
Proverbs 25:11

Like clouds and wind that bring no rain
are those who boast of gifts they never give.
Proverbs 25:14

Like someone who seizes a stray dog by the ears
is a person who meddles in someone else's quarrel.
Proverbs 26:17

As iron sharpens iron,
so one person sharpens the wits of another.
Proverbs 27:17

Just as you see your face reflected in water,
so your thoughts are reflected back to you by others.
Proverbs 27:19

Dead flies in sweet-smelling ointment make it smell bad,
so a little foolishness will make all your wisdom worthless.
Ecclesiastes 10:1

What else in God's big story
links up with this?

**Wisdom for
a New World**
p. 270

# The Wonderful Temple

Where's this in the Bible?

1 Kings 5–9

Solomon's father, King David, had wanted to build a house for God. It was to be a temple made of stone and wood, and it would replace the special tent where, till now, God had been living with his people. But God had told David he would not allow him to build the Temple because David had been too violent. Instead, God had promised that one of David's sons would build him a house.

That son was Solomon. First, Solomon assembled the finest building materials he could find, including the strongest stones and the best wood, as well as gold and precious stones from the hills around Jerusalem. Then he brought together the best builders and craftsmen he could find. All the special parts of the Temple, including the altar, the table, and the lampstand, were to be made of pure gold. Even the doors would be gold. The whole building was to be wonderful in every way.

It took seven years to build God's Temple, and when it was finished Solomon stood in front of the altar and led the people in prayer. Then he blessed the people and they had a big celebration. It lasted a whole week.

Solomon knew that God lived in heaven, but when Solomon had finished praying, God did something wonderful. Solomon and all the people looked up and saw the bright shining cloud of God's glory coming down from heaven and filling the Temple. And Solomon knew that heaven and earth were joined together.

God said to Solomon, "If you follow my rules and keep my law, I will live here among my people forever."

What else in God's big story links up with this?

**A Song of Hope and Joy**
p. 126

**New Temple, New Thinking**
p. 256

# A Visit from a Queen

Where's this in the Bible?

1 Kings 10–11

Solomon was the most famous king in all the world. He was incredibly wise and knew all there was to know. He taught the people all about the trees and plants, the stars and planets, the animals and birds. He understood why people thought the way they did, and why they did what they did. He understood what made good things good and bad things bad.

The Queen of Sheba heard of Solomon's wisdom and she travelled all the way from Africa to visit him. Her camel-trains carried presents: spices, gold, and precious stones. She listened to Solomon and asked him many questions. He answered them all. She saw his magnificent palace, the food and drink he had every day, his finely dressed servants, and the way he worshipped God in a beautiful temple.

"I had heard of you before," she said, "but they didn't tell me even half of it. What a wonderful place this is! Yahweh your God has blessed you indeed."

Solomon reigned for a long time. He began as a good and wise king, but when he was older his wisdom began to leave him. He married lots of wives from other nations. They came to live in his palace, and they brought with them their own gods. But instead of telling them about Yahweh, the true God, Solomon worshipped their gods as well.

That made God very sad. Solomon had broken God's special agreement and worshipped idols, and, because of that, Solomon's kingdom would end up being broken in two.

# The Kingdom is Broken in Two

Where's this in the Bible?

1 Kings 12–13

After Solomon died, his son Rehoboam became the king of Israel. In those days, Israel was made up of 12 large groups of people called tribes. Each of the 12 tribes was made up of families who were descended from one of the sons of Jacob.

Rehoboam began to rule over the 12 tribes. But not for long. He was a mean and bossy young man, and he treated the people badly. Soon most of the tribes decided they didn't want him as their king. Only the two tribes in the south, Judah and Benjamin, accepted him. The other ten tribes decided to go their own way and follow a different king. They chose Jeroboam, a man who had once been a servant in the palace of Solomon.

Jeroboam made the northern city of Shechem his new capital. Then, instead of worshipping God in the Temple in Jerusalem, Jeroboam did what Aaron had done long before. He made two golden statues of bulls. He put one in Bethel, in the middle of the country, and the other one in Dan, up in the north. Jeroboam said to the people, "These are your gods, who brought you out of Egypt!" He even started up a new festival, like the festivals Moses had started years ago.

From that day, the kingdom of David and Solomon was broken in two. Jeroboam's kingdom, Israel, was in the north, and Rehoboam's kingdom, Judah, was in the south.

God was very sad that this had happened. He sent a prophet to warn Jeroboam that he would be punished because he had turned so many of the people away from God.

What else in God's big story links up with this?

**Aaron Makes an Idol**

p. 46

# Hosea's Warning

Where's this in the Bible?

Hosea 1–2, 11, 14

When God had made his special agreement with Israel, it was like a marriage. God was like a husband, and Israel was like a wife. That was their special agreement. But Jeroboam had led the northern tribes away from Yahweh and had made them worship idols. That was like a wife abandoning her husband and going off to live with a different man.

God wanted the northern tribes to know how sad he was that the people had broken his agreement. So God found a prophet, Hosea, and told him to do something that would show the people how he felt. God told Hosea to marry a woman who would love him at first, but later she would leave him for someone else.

Poor Hosea. He loved his wife, and they were happy together for a while. But later, when his wife left him, Hosea felt so sad and lonely. He told the people how he had been abandoned. Then he told them how they had abandoned God in the same way, and how God felt sad and lonely too. But even though the people had turned away from him, God still loved them and wanted them back.

God could remember how wonderful it had been when he brought his people out of Egypt. He wanted it to be like that again. So Hosea warned Israel that their rebellion would end in trouble. What they had to do now was come back to God and say sorry.

If Israel did that, God would forgive them, and they would flourish. They would be like a lovely plant, with deep roots and spreading branches, giving off a delightful scent and providing shade for the garden.

# Elijah and the Prophets of Baal

Where's this in the Bible?

1 Kings 18–19

Once, there was another king who led Israel away from God. His name was Ahab. He and his wife Jezebel worshipped Baal instead of Yahweh. They even had a large group of servants who called themselves "the prophets of Baal".

One day, God sent his own prophet, Elijah, to tell the people that all this idol-worship had to stop. But they wouldn't listen. So Elijah challenged the prophets of Baal to a contest. First, they had to build an altar and pray for their god to send fire on the sacrifice. The prophets of Baal prayed all day. "Oh Baal, hear us!" they cried. But no answer came, and no fire either. Then it was Elijah's turn. First he built an altar and prepared the sacrifice. Then he dug a deep trench around the altar and poured water all over it. The people looking on thought he was mad! Then, calmly and quietly, Elijah knelt and prayed to Yahweh.

Suddenly, a huge ball of flames flashed through the sky! The fire licked up all the water and everything was burned to a cinder. All the people were amazed. They fell to their knees and worshipped Yahweh. It was clear who had won the contest.

When Ahab and Jezebel heard what had happened, they were furious. They wanted to kill Elijah, but he ran away into the desert. He went for many miles until he came to Mount Sinai, where God had appeared to Moses many years before. When Elijah reached the mountain, a huge storm began to swirl around it. There was a howling wind, a terrible earthquake, and a raging fire! But Yahweh wasn't in any of them. Then Elijah heard a small, quiet voice, and he knew that it was Yahweh. "Go back," said God. "You will find a young man called Elisha. He will take over from you as my prophet."

What else in God's big story links up with this?

**On God's Mountain**
p. 44

# Elisha Helps an Enemy

Where's this
in the Bible?

1 Kings 19;
2 Kings 2, 5

Elijah did as God had said. He went and found Elisha, and taught him to be a prophet. Elisha said to Elijah, "I want to be a holy man like you."

"Hmm. That's hard," said Elijah, "but one day, when I'm taken from you, perhaps you'll get what you've asked for."

One day, as Elijah and Elisha were walking together, God sent a chariot of fire to take Elijah to heaven. The chariot swept Elijah away in a whirlwind, and as he flew up in the chariot he dropped his cloak. Elisha picked it up and put it on, and from that day he became a powerful prophet like Elijah, healing the sick and feeding the hungry.

In those days, a powerful nation called Aram used to attack Israel. The commander of the Aramean army, Naaman, had a bad skin disease. It covered his whole body. Naaman had tried everything to get rid of it, but it wouldn't go away. He had almost given up when one of his servants, a young girl, told him about Elisha. Naaman decided to visit the prophet, hoping that he would perform a great miracle. But all Elisha did was tell him to go and wash seven times in the River Jordan. Naaman was annoyed. "Why should I do that?" he shouted. "We have better rivers in Aram!" But before going home, he did what Elisha had said, and straight away he was cured.

After that, Naaman knew that Yahweh, Israel's God, was the only true God. He would try to worship Yahweh back home in Aram. It would be difficult, but he would try.

What else in God's big story
links up with this?

**God's Kingdom
is Coming!**
p. 152

# Isaiah's Vision of Yahweh

Where's this in the Bible?

Isaiah 6

God was very disappointed with the northern tribes for the way they kept turning away from him. But the people of Judah in the south were hardly any better. Their kings were weak, and they failed to lead the people in God's ways.

One day, a young man called Isaiah went into the Temple in Jerusalem, the capital of Judah. There he saw something so awesome it took his breath away. He saw a vision of Yahweh himself! He was sitting high up on a throne, with fiery angels all around him. The bright cloud of God's glory filled the whole building, and the angels were singing:

"Holy, holy, holy is Yahweh the leader!
His glory fills the earth."

Isaiah was terrified. No sinful person could see God and live. Then, one of the angels took a burning coal from the altar and touched Isaiah's lips with it. "This has taken away your sin," said the angel.

Then Isaiah heard God speaking. "Who shall I send?" asked God. "Who will speak for me?"

"Here am I," replied Isaiah. "Send me."

God replied, "Very well. Go to the people and tell them that trouble is coming. They will hear but they won't want to understand. They will be like a tree that has been chopped down. But there will be holy life in the stump of the tree, and one day the tree will grow back."

What else in God's big story links up with this?

**On the Road to Damascus**
p. 238

**John's Vision of Jesus**
p. 276

# Good King Hezekiah

Where's this in the Bible?

2 Kings 18–19

After his vision in the Temple, Isaiah became a great prophet. He told the people of Judah to stop worshipping idols. If they didn't, it would only bring trouble. Then, after many years, the trouble started to happen. The king of Assyria, the most powerful nation on earth, sent his army to attack the kingdom of Israel. But it didn't stop there. The Assyrian army carried on marching southwards, down toward the little kingdom of Judah.

At that time, a king called Hezekiah ruled in Jerusalem. Hezekiah tried to persuade the king of Assyria to call off his army by offering him gold and silver. But the Assyrian king just laughed at him.

When the huge Assyrian army arrived at the walls of Jerusalem, the people were very frightened. King Hezekiah had sent some soldiers to the battlements above the city gates. The Assyrians sent a messenger, who shouted up to them, "We command you to surrender! Don't listen to Hezekiah. We have captured all the other cities in Judah, and we will take Jerusalem too."

The messenger then sent the same message to the king in a letter. When Hezekiah saw the letter, he went into God's Temple. He spread out the letter before God and knelt down to pray. "They are laughing at you," he said. "But you are Yahweh, the only true God. Please, save us!"

When God heard that, he sent the prophet Isaiah to tell Hezekiah that Jerusalem would be safe. And so, that very night, Hezekiah's prayer was answered. A deadly plague spread throughout the Assyrian army. Thousands of men died. The Assyrian king was no longer laughing. He went home to his palace, and shortly afterwards he died too.

# The Forgotten Book

Where's this in the Bible?

2 Kings 22–23; Jeremiah 25

As time went by, the people of Jerusalem forgot about God and all he had done for them. God's Temple no longer looked wonderful. It had fallen into disrepair and was looking unloved and neglected.

But there was one king, Josiah, who decided things had to change. He gave orders for the Temple to be repaired and tried to get everything working again. The people needed to worship and serve God properly. Then, one day, while the repairs were going on, one of the priests found a large scroll hidden away inside the Temple. It was very old and covered in thick dust. The priest wondered what it could be. But when he unrolled it, he realized what he was holding! It was the Law of Moses, including the special agreement that God had made with his people hundreds of years before. It had been lying there for years, forgotten and unopened.

When the priest showed the scroll to King Josiah, he was horrified. The scroll made it clear that if God's people disobeyed, trouble would come upon them. So the king tried to make everything right again. He got the priests to remove the idols that had been placed inside the Temple. He destroyed all the altars of Baal. And he made the people promise to worship Yahweh and obey his rules.

Josiah had done what he could, but it wasn't long before the people forgot God again and went back to their old ways. So God sent a prophet, Jeremiah, who told them, "It's no good patching things up on the outside. What matters is your heart: whether you're truly worshipping God and looking after the poor and needy." Jeremiah warned them that a time of great trouble was coming. Jerusalem would be attacked and destroyed, and the people would be forced to live in exile, far away from Jerusalem, in a foreign land. Then, eventually, God would change their hearts so that they could really be his people at last.

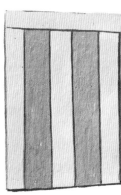

# God Abandons the Temple

Where's this in the Bible?

Ezekiel 10

From the time of David and Solomon, God had promised to live with his people in the Temple in Jerusalem. But now, most of the people didn't care about God anymore, not even the priests who were meant to lead them. Instead they worshipped idols, and they were selfish, hateful, and cruel to others.

But there was one good priest, who was also a prophet. His name was Ezekiel. One day, Ezekiel had a terrifying vision. In his vision he could see the Temple in Jerusalem. Then he saw something that made him tremble. A huge bright shining cloud was coming out of the Temple, and in the cloud he saw some strange-looking angels, with wheels whizzing round beside them.

Ezekiel looked harder, and saw that the angels were carrying a throne, made like a chariot. Ezekiel looked even harder, and what he saw made him tremble even more. Riding on the throne-chariot, surrounded by the bright cloud, was God himself! Ezekiel watched the throne-chariot, angels and wheels, and all, rise up into the sky above the Mount of Olives, and disappear into the distance.

Ezekiel knew what it meant. God had had enough. The people, and the priests who were supposed to lead them, had become so bad that God could no longer live among them.

Now the Temple was empty. God had abandoned it. The enemy would be able to capture it at last.

What else in God's big story links up with this?

**Jesus and the Temple**
p. 198

**A Song for Everyone!**
p. 278

# Exile!

Where's this in the Bible?

2 Kings 25; Psalm 137:3, 42:1, 142:7

The words of Jeremiah and all the prophets came true. They had warned the people what would happen, just as Moses had warned the Israelites hundreds of years before.

And so it was that the army of Babylon, which was now the most powerful nation on earth, marched into Judah, surrounded Jerusalem, and attacked it.

The Babylonians showed no mercy. They captured the king of Judah and killed his sons. They burned the Temple to the ground. Then they took the king himself and deported him to Babylon, and most of the people with him.

The people of Judah hated living in exile, hundreds of miles from home. The Babylonians used to mock them. "Why don't you sing us some of your nice songs?" they would say. "Like the ones you used to sing in your Temple!"

As the years went by, the people thought more and more about what they had lost. It seemed as though Yahweh had abandoned them forever. They felt like animals in the desert, longing for a cool spring of water. They cried because people they loved had been killed. They bowed their heads because it seemed they had no hope.

They used to pray that God would make it all right again. But they couldn't see how. It was like being in a dark prison with no windows.

They knew that this was what God had warned them would happen, but they couldn't see how that helped.

What else in God's big story links up with this?

**The World
Goes Wrong**
p. 8

**Promises and
Warnings**
p. 58

# Daniel and His Friends

Where's this in the Bible?

Daniel 1–3

A young man called Daniel and his three friends were among the people who had been captured and taken to Babylon. The king of Babylon tried to make them eat food that was forbidden by God's law. They refused and ate only vegetables, but they grew fitter and stronger than everybody else. God gave them wisdom, and to Daniel he also gave the ability to explain the meaning of dreams and visions.

One night, the king of Babylon dreamed he saw a huge statue of a man. It was made from four kinds of metal. It had a golden head, silver chest and arms, bronze body, iron legs, and feet made from a mixture of iron and clay. Suddenly, a stone appeared and smashed the statue's feet, bringing it crashing down and smashing it to bits. Then the stone got bigger and bigger until it became an enormous mountain that filled the whole earth. Daniel explained the dream. There would be four great empires, beginning with the empire of Babylon. But, in the end, God would set up a new kingdom that would fill the whole earth and last forever.

Some time later, the king built a huge statue made of gold. He ordered everyone to worship it. Anyone who didn't would be thrown into a blazing fire. But Daniel's three friends refused. "We worship Yahweh," they said. "We will never bow down to a statue." So the king ordered his soldiers to throw them into the fire. He expected them to die, but when he peered into the roaring flames he saw something incredible. There were the three young men, alive and well and without a mark on them! Not only that, when he looked again he could see a fourth person talking with the three friends as the flames leaped up around them. Then the king realized that God had sent an angel to rescue them. The king called the young men out of the fire and praised them for being so brave.

They had stayed loyal to Yahweh, and they had been ready to die rather than worship an idol.

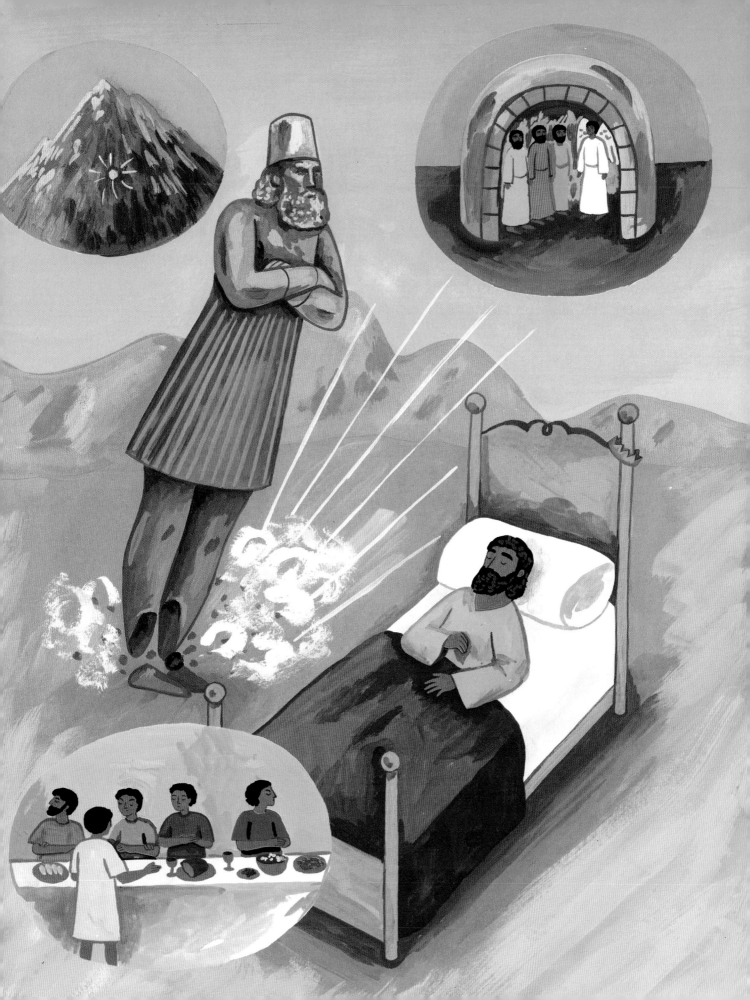

# Daniel and the Monsters

Where's this in the Bible?

Daniel 5–7

The years went by and a new king took over the kingdom of Babylon. Daniel had continued to grow in wisdom, and the new king made him his special advisor. That made the other royal advisors envious. They huddled together and whispered to each other. "We don't like the way the king listens to Daniel and not to us," they said. "Let's find a way to get him into trouble."

First, they made up a new law and got the king to approve it. The law said that everyone had to pray to the king himself and to nobody else, and that anyone who didn't would be thrown into a pit full of hungry lions. Next, they spied on Daniel to see what he would do. When they found Daniel praying to God as he had always done, they said to the king, "Daniel has continued to worship his god and refuses to worship you."

Their plan worked. Even though the king liked Daniel, he had to apply the law he had made. So Daniel was arrested and thrown to the lions. The next morning the king hurried to the lion pit and called out hopefully, "Daniel, has your God saved you?" And there was Daniel, alive and well, without a mark on him! So the king brought Daniel up out of the pit. He sent a message out to all the world, declaring that Daniel's god, Yahweh, was the only true god.

Daniel was a great prophet and God sent him many visions. In one vision, Daniel saw four horrible monsters came up out of the sea, shouting terrible threats. But then Daniel saw a great king sitting on a throne in heaven. This heavenly king was called "the Ancient of Days". Next, a human being came up to the king and sat beside him. The human being was called a "Son of Man". The monsters were condemned to death, and the "Son of Man" became king of the whole world.

What else in God's big story links up with this?

**Jesus is Put on Trial**
p. 210

THE OLD TESTAMENT

# God Promises to Rescue His People

Where's this in the Bible?

Isaiah 40;
Jeremiah 31;
Ezekiel 36, 37

The people of Judah who had been deported to Babylon thought their exile would never end. So God sent prophets to comfort them and tell them that their punishment wouldn't last forever. God would forgive them and one day he would bring them back to their land.

The prophet Isaiah promised that God himself would come back to rescue his people. The people of Jerusalem would see him coming. He would overthrow the gods of Babylon and prove that he was the world's true king.

The prophet Jeremiah promised that God would make a new agreement with his people. He would renew their hearts, so that they would love him and serve him in a new way.

The prophet Ezekiel promised that God would wash his people from their sins, inside and out, and change their hearts so that they would love him and serve him.

Ezekiel told the people about a mysterious vision he had seen. He found himself in a dark valley. As he looked around he noticed that the valley was full of human bones, scattered all over the ground. Then he heard a voice, saying, "Can these dry bones live?" God told Ezekiel to prophesy to the bones, and when he did that the bones began to move! Then they began to connect with each other, forming human skeletons. Then they grew muscles, skin, and hair. Then, when they were fully formed, God's breath came into them, and they got up and walked about!

When the vision had ended, Ezekiel realized that God was telling him something wonderful. God was revealing that his people would be renewed and made strong and whole again, like dead people coming back to life.

What else in God's big story links up with this?

**The Father Who Forgave**
p. 186

**God's New Agreement**
p. 268

# The Suffering Servant

Where's this in the Bible?

Isaiah 42, 49, 50, 52–53, 54, 55

The prophet Isaiah was sent by God to remind the people that they were supposed to be God's servants. But instead of serving God, they had turned away from him and broken his special agreement. God had always warned them what would happen if they did this, and so they had found themselves in exile.

While they were still in exile, God sent a prophet to tell them that one day soon God would come alongside them, to comfort and rescue them. God would send someone special: God's own true servant. God would put his own spirit inside him, so that he could make everything right and show the people the way back to God.

The servant would share the sufferings of God's people, so that at first it would look as though he had failed. He would suffer terrible things and die. All the sin and evil in the world would be heaped upon him, and it would kill him. His wounds, his bruises, and his death would be the punishment God's people had deserved. The servant would take their punishment instead of them.

But afterwards God would give his servant new life! The servant would be raised up, and it would be clear to all the world that he had been doing what God wanted all along.

After that, God would welcome his people back again. Not only that, God would open up his promises to everyone. There would be a new agreement! It would be like the Garden of Eden all over again, but now it would be open to people from anywhere in the world.

What else in God's big story links up with this?

**Death in the Vineyard**
p. 200

**Jesus is Crucified**
p. 216

# Rebuilding Jerusalem

Where's this in the Bible?

Ezra 1, 7, 10;
Nehemiah 1–2, 8–9

The people of Judah who had been taken to Babylon lived there in exile for seventy years. Toward the end of that time, the king of Persia conquered the king of Babylon and took over his empire. The empire of Persia now ruled everywhere, including the land that had once belonged to the people of Judah: the land that came to be called "Judea".

That was when God decided it was time to act. God told the king of Persia to allow some of the exiled Judeans to go back to Judea and rebuild the Temple in Jerusalem. Lots of the Judeans were very excited when they heard this news. They got their families and belongings together and made the long journey back to the Promised Land. They began to settle back in the towns and villages around Jerusalem, and some of them began to rebuild the Temple.

But not all the people had learned the lessons from before. There were still some who were not living in the way God wanted. So God sent a man called Ezra to explain to the people in Jerusalem what they had to do. Ezra had studied the Law of Moses all his life. He was eager to help others learn how to follow it and to live as God's people.

A few years later, God sent another leader to Jerusalem. His name was Nehemiah. His job was to lead the people in rebuilding the city wall, which still lay in ruins. Then, when the work was complete, Nehemiah and Ezra led the people in saying sorry to God for all the things that had gone wrong.

# When Will God Return?

Where's this in the Bible?

Zechariah 4;
Malachi 1–4

After the Temple had been rebuilt, the people were wondering when Yahweh would come back to dwell in it. "When will we see God's glory again?" they asked each other.

The prophet Zechariah promised the people that God would indeed return. He gave them this message from God: "It won't happen by ordinary power. It will happen by my Spirit."

But the priests in charge of the Temple were losing patience and getting bored. "Why should we bother doing all these sacrifices if God isn't going to return?" they asked.

The prophet Malachi spoke firmly to them. "One day all the world will worship God," he said. "So you must make sure to do it properly now."

Malachi also warned the men of Judea against sending their Judean wives away and marrying others instead. They had to remain as God's special people. What's more, God was going to send a messenger to prepare the way for the day when he would himself return to dwell with them.

The people needed to get ready.

What else in God's big story links up with this?

**Jesus is Baptized**
p. 148

**Jesus Enters Jerusalem**
p. 196

# A Song of Hope and Joy

Where's this
in the Bible?

Psalm 84

*In this poem, one of God's people looks forward with joy to the day when they will worship God in the Temple once again.*

Yahweh, we love your dwelling place.
Your Temple gives us joy.
Your presence to enjoy.

The lucky birds can make their nests
In gardens all nearby.
They lay their eggs and hatch their young
Beside your altars high.

The singers love to praise your name
They worship day by day.
The pilgrims, too, they think of you
Along their winding way.

So be with us, Yahweh our God.
Be sure to bless our king.
I'd rather work within your house
Than almost anything.

Yahweh, you are a sun and shield.
You give us all we need.
It's such a blessing to be here
And on your love to feed.

What else in God's big story
links up with this?

**The Wonderful
Temple**
p. 92

THE OLD TESTAMENT

# Esther Rescues Her People

Where's this in the Bible?

Esther 1–8

The king of Persia wanted a new queen. All the beautiful young women in his kingdom were brought to him. The one he chose was Esther. She was a Judean. Her family had been brought there from Jerusalem, but her parents were now dead, and she lived with her guardian, Mordecai.

One day Mordecai discovered some men plotting to kill the king. He told Queen Esther, and she told the king. The plot was foiled. But Haman, one of the king's officials, hated the Judeans. He planned to have them all killed, and he was going to start with Mordecai. Esther was worried. She knew that Haman planned to have her guardian executed, but what could she do to protect him? And what could she do to stop her people being killed?

Esther told her friends to pray. Then, that night, the king could not sleep, and he asked his servants to read him the stories of what had happened in his reign. And he remembered how Mordecai had saved his life.

Then Esther invited Haman to a special feast at the king's palace. It would be just the three of them. Haman felt very proud to be there. But when the feast was nearly over, Esther told the king, "Haman has been plotting behind your back to kill my people." The king's face turned red with anger, and Haman became very frightened. The king jumped up from the table and stormed out of the palace in a rage! Haman's face turned pale with fright.

Haman was right to be scared. The king ordered him to be executed instead of Mordecai. Then the king declared that the Judeans should be allowed to take up arms and defend themselves from their enemies.

# Jonah and the Giant Fish

Where's this in the Bible?

Jonah 1–4

There was once a prophet called Jonah. God told him to go to Nineveh, the capital city of Assyria. He had to warn the people there that God was angry with them. But Jonah didn't like this idea, and instead of going to Nineveh he got on a ship going the other way. After a while a great storm blew up. The ship was going to sink! The sailors tried to save the ship, but it was no good. Then Jonah told the sailors, "It's my fault. I'm trying to run away from God. If you throw me overboard, the storm will stop and you'll be saved."

And that's just what happened. The sailors threw Jonah into the raging sea and straight away the storm stopped. Then, to save Jonah from drowning, God sent a giant fish to swallow him up! Jonah was in the fish's stomach for three days and nights. He prayed that God would rescue him, and finally the fish spat him out onto dry land.

For a second time, God told Jonah to go to Nineveh, and this time Jonah obeyed. He walked along their streets, declaring, "Unless you stop all the bad things you're doing, God will destroy your city!" At this, the Ninevites stopped and prayed for forgiveness, and God decided not to punish them after all. But Jonah was still angry with the Ninevites. He wanted his prophecy to come true, and he thought God should destroy them all anyway! So he went up a hill, looking over the city. He sat down in the shade of a tree and waited to see what would happen.

God decided to teach Jonah a lesson. He sent a worm to attack the tree. The tree was soon destroyed, and now Jonah had no shade. The heat of the sun beat down on Jonah, and that made the prophet's anger even hotter! Then God said, "Jonah, are you sad because you've lost the tree? How do you think I would feel if I lost all those people in that city?"

# The Promise of a New World

Where's this
in the Bible?

Isaiah 11, 35, 55, 65

The prophet Isaiah saw wonderful visions of God's new world.

Yahweh would send a new, wise king. Under his rule, everything wrong in the world would be put right. He would rescue poor, helpless people from those who hated and hurt them.

Wild animals would become tame. Dangerous beasts would become safe. They would live together in peace, with a little child looking after them.

Deserts would grow beautiful flowers. People who had been blind would see, people who had been deaf would hear, and people with physical disabilities would dance for joy.

God's people would return to their own land. They would live in peace.

In fact, God would make a new heaven and a new earth. Yahweh's glorious presence would fill this newborn world, like the water filling the sea.

Everybody, all over the world, would be invited to a great feast.

Just as it was in the beginning, when the world began, God would speak and at his word it would be done.

What else in God's big story links up with this?

**The Garden of Eden**
p. 4

**New Heaven,
New Earth**
p. 280

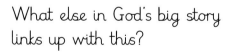
THE OLD TESTAMENT

132

# Praise to the King of Kings!

Where's this in the Bible?

Psalm 72

*This poem looks forward to the time when God's chosen king will bring justice and peace to the whole world, and God's glory will fill the earth.*

Yahweh, give justice to the king!
Enable him to judge the right.
Let him decide with equity.
Let him defend the poor with might.

Send to us now, from highest hills,
The rivers of abundant peace.
May justice flow through all the land.
Confront oppression, let it cease!

From sea to sea his reign shall spread
And distant kings their gifts shall bring.
His enemies shall lick the dust,
The needy poor his praise shall sing.

Praise be to Yahweh, Israel's God!
For only he can do these things.
His glory now shall flood the world
And all adore the King of Kings.

What else in God's big story links up with this?

**Gifts for a King**
p. 144

**God's Kingdom is Coming!**
p. 152

# Part Two

God's Story in the New Testament

# Zechariah and the Angel

Where's this in the Bible?

Luke 1

Zechariah was a priest. He and his wife Elizabeth were sad because they had no children. For many years they had hoped and prayed for a child, but now they were too old.

One day, Zechariah was working in the Temple in Jerusalem when suddenly he saw an angel standing next to him! Zechariah was frightened, and he started to back away. Then the angel spoke.

"Don't be afraid. God has heard your prayer. Your wife Elizabeth will have a son, and you must call him 'John'. He will be a great prophet, filled with God's Spirit, and he will guide the people back to God."

Zechariah couldn't believe it. "How can this happen?" he exclaimed. "Elizabeth and I are far too old!"

"I am Gabriel," said the angel. "I stand in God's presence. Now, because you didn't believe me, you won't be able to speak again until it happens." With that, the angel disappeared. And so did Zechariah's voice.

The weeks went by, and then one day Elizabeth said to Zechariah, "We're going to have a baby!" Zechariah's face glowed with happiness, but still he couldn't speak.

Later that year, the baby was born. It was a boy! Friends and relatives from all around came to celebrate. They knew this must be a very special child, and they asked what his name would be. Zechariah beckoned for a writing tablet. Everything went quiet and they all watched as he wrote, "His name is John." And suddenly Zechariah could speak again! He sang a song of praise to God, and everyone laughed and danced for joy.

*What else in God's big story links up with this?*

**Hannah's Special Child**
p. 70

# Mary Has a Special Visitor

Where's this in the Bible?

Luke 1

A few months after visiting Zechariah in the Temple, the angel Gabriel was sent by God to a small house in Nazareth, a town far to the north of Jerusalem in the region of Galilee. Gabriel was going to give some special news to a young woman called Mary. Mary was Elizabeth's cousin. She was going to marry Joseph, who was descended from King David.

The news that Gabriel was bringing to Mary was going to change her life. More than that, it was going to change the whole world. Forever!

Mary was frightened when she saw the angel. "Don't be afraid!" said Gabriel. "God is with you. You're going to have a baby! His name will be Jesus. He will be the king of Israel, and his kingdom will last forever!"

"How can this happen?" asked Mary. "I'm not even married!"

"God's Holy Spirit inside you will make it happen," explained Gabriel. "Your child will be God's own son. To show you what God can do, your cousin Elizabeth is going to have a baby too, even though she's old."

Mary bowed her head. "Here I am," she said. "I am God's servant. May it happen, just as you have said."

After Gabriel had left, Mary decided to visit Elizabeth. When she was near the house, Elizabeth hurried out to meet her and the two women gave each other a joyful hug. They were so excited! Then Mary sang a beautiful song of thanks to God. She stayed with Elizabeth for three months, before going back home to Nazareth.

What else in God's big story links up with this?

**God Makes a Special Agreement**
p. 18

# Jesus is Born!

Where's this in the Bible?

Luke 2

In those days Judea was part of an empire that was ruled by a powerful king who lived in the city of Rome. The Romans called their king "Caesar". Judea was part of his empire. It still had its own king, but it was Caesar who gave the orders and made sure the Judean king did what he wanted.

Around that time, an order came from Rome saying that everyone in the empire had to be counted. This meant Mary and Joseph had to go to Bethlehem, where Joseph's family had come from. They packed their bags and got ready for the long journey south. But by the time they reached Bethlehem, all the inns were full and there was nowhere left for them to stay.

What could they do? Mary was ready to have her baby, and they had to find somewhere quickly! In the end they rested in a place where animals were kept. That night, Mary's baby was born. After feeding him, she wrapped him up snugly, and gently laid him in the animals' feeding trough.

Meanwhile, on the hills outside the town, some shepherds were looking after their sheep. All was calm, when suddenly an angel appeared to them. The bright light of God's glory shone all around. "Don't be afraid," said the angel. "I bring you good news! God's true king has been born in Bethlehem. If you want to see him, you'll find him asleep in a feeding trough!" Then the whole sky was full of angels, singing praises to God.

After the angels had gone, the shepherds hurried to Bethlehem. At last they found the baby. He was fast asleep in a feeding trough, just as the angel had said. The shepherds told everyone what they had seen. And Mary remembered it all. She hid it away in her heart.

What else in God's big story links up with this?

**God's Promise to David**
p. 82

# Gifts for a King

Where's this
in the Bible?

Matthew 2

Far away in the East, some wise men were studying the stars. The stars told them that a new king had been born. They wanted to see this king, so they got on their camels and followed a bright star that led them to Jerusalem. There they found a big palace, and in the palace was the king of Judea. His name was Herod. The wise men asked to see the newborn king, but when Herod heard that, he became alarmed. "What's all this about?" he thought. "I'm the only king around here!"

"Your majesty," said one of Herod's men, "the ancient prophecies are clear. The king that these men are looking for will not be born in Jerusalem, but in Bethlehem, the city of David." Herod took the wise men to one side, an evil glint in his eye. "All right, then," he said. "Why don't you go and find this king, and then please come back and tell me where he is."

So the wise men mounted their camels and set off for Bethlehem, still following the star. They came to a house, and in the house were Mary and Joseph and the baby Jesus. The wise men knelt and kissed the baby's tiny feet. Then they gave him three special gifts: gold, frankincense, and myrrh.

Soon it was time for the men to leave, but instead of going back to Herod, they went home by a different way. God had sent them a dream, warning them that Herod wanted to find the baby and kill him. Eventually, Herod realized that the wise men weren't coming back. But by then it was too late. Jesus had already escaped!

God had told Joseph to take Mary and Jesus to Egypt, where they lived as refugees from Herod. They stayed in Egypt until news reached them that Herod was dead. Then they knew it was safe to make the long journey back to their homeland.

What else in God's big story links up with this?

**Praise to the
King of Kings!**
p. 134

# Jesus Goes Missing

Where's this
in the Bible?

Luke 2

Mary and Joseph were happy to be back in Galilee. Joseph worked as a builder, and as Jesus grew older he helped his father in his workshop. The Romans were building a new city nearby, so Joseph was kept very busy.

Every year, Joseph would take his family on a special journey to Jerusalem, where they would celebrate the festival of Passover with lots of other people. The festival of Passover reminded them that God had rescued his people from slavery in Egypt and that one day he would rescue them again.

When Jesus was 12, he went with his family to Jerusalem to celebrate Passover. They had a wonderful time, and when it was over they set off for home. Mary and Joseph thought Jesus was with the other boys and girls who were travelling with them. But he wasn't! They called out for him: "Jesus, where are you?" But there was no reply.

Mary and Joseph dashed back to Jerusalem in a panic. They searched for Jesus everywhere, knocking on doors and asking everyone if they had seen him. Then, after three days of frantic searching, they found him. He was in the Temple with the teachers, listening and asking questions.

Jesus' parents had been so worried about him. "How could you do this to us?" said Mary, with tears in her eyes. Jesus replied, "Didn't you know that I would be busy in my Father's house?"

Mary and Joseph looked at each other. They weren't sure that they understood what Jesus meant, but they were glad he was safe. "Come on," said Joseph. "Let's go home."

# Jesus is Baptized

Where's this in the Bible?

Matthew 3

Many years later, when he had grown into a man, Jesus made the journey south from Galilee to Judea. He had heard that his cousin, John, had become a great prophet. People were calling him John the Baptist.

John was getting the people ready for God to come back and rescue them. He taught them how to turn away from selfishness and sinful living and follow God's ways instead. To show them what this meant, he called the people into the desert, where he would plunge them, one by one, into the River Jordan. (That's why John became known as John the Baptist: to baptize something means to plunge it under water.) As John lifted each person back out of the water, their sins were washed away and they were reminded of the time when God saved his people from slavery in Egypt.

John told the people: "I am baptizing you with water, but someone more powerful than me will come. He will baptize you with God's Holy Spirit and with fire." The people wondered who this person could be.

One day, as John was teaching the people, Jesus came and asked to be baptized. When John saw Jesus, he said, "I should be baptized by you, not the other way round!" But Jesus insisted, and so John plunged Jesus into the water. As Jesus came back up, God's hidden world of heaven was suddenly opened! People could see right in. They looked on in amazement as God's Spirit came from heaven and settled on Jesus like a dove.

Then they heard a voice, saying to Jesus, "You are my son! You are the one I love! You make me very glad!"

What else in God's big story links up with this?

**A Journey through the Sea**

p. 40

THE NEW TESTAMENT

148

# Jesus Goes into the Desert

Where's this in the Bible?

Matthew 4

After John had baptized him, Jesus was taken by God's Spirit into the desert. Jesus was there, with no food, for 40 days and 40 nights. He was tired, and very hungry. Then he heard a voice. It was soft and tempting.

"If you are God's Son," whispered the voice, "tell these stones to become bread!"

Jesus shook his head. "The Bible tells us to feed on God's word," he said, "not just bread."

"If you really are God's Son," said the tempter, "why not throw yourself off the high tower in the Temple? Angels will save you, and then everyone will see that God is looking after you."

"No," replied Jesus. "The Bible says we mustn't test God!"

Then the tempter showed Jesus all the wonderful kingdoms of the world. "These can all be yours!" said the tempter. "I'll give them to you. All you have to do is fall down and worship me."

"Get away from me!" said Jesus. "The Bible says, worship the Lord your God. Serve him and him alone!"

After he had overcome the tempter, Jesus returned to Galilee and began to tell the people there, "Now is the time! At last God is becoming king!"

What else in God's big story links up with this?

**The World Goes Wrong**
p. 8

**Promises and Warnings**
p. 58

# God's Kingdom is Coming!

Where's this in the Bible?

Luke 4

When Jesus was in Galilee, lots of people with diseases came to see him. Jesus felt love for them, so he began to heal them with power from God and to teach them about God's kingdom.

One day, he visited Nazareth, where he had grown up. He went into the synagogue, a place where people gathered to worship God and read from the Bible. When it was time for the Bible reading, Jesus went to the front and read out these words written by the prophet Isaiah:

"The spirit of the Lord is upon me!
Because of him I can tell the good news to the poor.
Prisoners will be released, blind people will see.
And those who are treated unjustly will be set free."

Then Jesus said, "These words are coming true today!" And he explained what the "good news" would mean for everyone. But the people were alarmed. Was Jesus really saying that God was going to do good things for everyone, even for their enemies?

"Well," said Jesus, "God doesn't only care about good people, you know. In the days of the prophet Elisha there were lots of people in Israel who had diseases, but God didn't send Elisha to them. Instead, he healed the commander of the enemy army."

When they heard that, the people in the synagogue became very angry. They wanted to grab Jesus and kill him! But Jesus calmly walked away and escaped. He went to live in Capernaum, a town near a big lake called the Sea of Galilee. There he carried on teaching and healing, and many people went to see him.

What else in God's big story links up with this?

**Praise to the King of Kings!**
p. 134

# Twelve Special Followers

Where's this in the Bible?

Matthew 4, 19

One day, Jesus was walking beside the Sea of Galilee when he saw two fishermen casting their nets into the sea. They were brothers: Peter and Andrew. Jesus called out to them, "Follow me! I'll have you fishing for people!" Straight away they stopped what they were doing and followed him.

Jesus walked on until he saw two more fishermen. They too were brothers: James and John. They were sitting in a boat mending some fishing nets. Jesus called to them as well, and straight away they stopped what they were doing and followed him.

Lots of people wanted to follow Jesus, but he chose just 12 to be his special, closest followers. The closest of all were Peter, James, and John. Jesus called his special followers "disciples". A disciple is someone who devotes their life to understanding what their leader is saying and doing. They try to follow the leader's example in every way.

There was a reason why Jesus chose 12 disciples, and not 11 or 13. Long ago, when the people of Israel became a nation, they were grouped into 12 tribes. But years later the people were attacked by foreign armies and taken into exile. Later still, some of the people returned to their homeland, but the 12 tribes had never come back together as a whole nation. So, when Jesus chose 12 disciples, he was showing people that God was bringing Israel together in a new way. "In God's new world," he said, "you who have followed me will sit on 12 thrones and rule over the 12 tribes of Israel!"

# Wine for a Wedding Feast

Where's this in the Bible?

John 2

Around that time, Jesus and his mother, Mary, were invited to a wedding. Some of Jesus' disciples came too. The wedding feast was going well and everyone was having fun. Servants were busy serving the food and drink, when one of them noticed that all the wine was gone!

Mary found Jesus. "There's no more wine," she said.

"Mother," said Jesus, "what do you want me to do about that?"

Mary gave Jesus a knowing look. Then she found some servants and told them to do whatever Jesus said. Jesus told them to fill six large jars with water, right up to the top. Then he told them to pour some into a cup and take it to the man in charge of the feast.

When the man tasted what was in the cup, he was amazed. "What's this?" he asked. "I thought the wine had run out!"

He didn't know where the new wine had come from, but he did know that it was the best wine he'd ever tasted. So he called the bridegroom over to taste it too.

The bridegroom took a sip. The wine was so good, he could hardly believe his tastebuds. "Well, that's strange," said the man in charge. "Normally, people serve the best wine first and bring out the cheaper wine later, when no one will notice. But, judging by the taste of this, you've kept the best wine till last!"

Everyone was amazed at what they saw. Jesus was showing what it looked like when God's power and glory were revealed.

# Jesus Heals a Paralyzed Man

Where's this in the Bible?

Luke 5

One day, a crowd of people had gathered in a house to hear Jesus teach. Four men came up to the house. They had a friend who was paralyzed. He couldn't walk, so his friends carried him around on a stretcher. The men were looking for Jesus. They wanted him to heal their friend, but they couldn't get into the house because of the crowd. Then they had an idea. They climbed onto the roof of the house, pulling their friend up after them on his stretcher. Inside the house the crowd were gathered, listening to Jesus. "What's that noise?" said someone. Everyone stopped and looked up. Four faces were peering down at them through a hole in the roof.

"There's Jesus!" whispered one of the men from above. "Quick, lower the stretcher."

Jesus knew at once what the men were trying to do, and that they really believed he could heal the man on the stretcher. So, as the man was being let down into the room, Jesus said to him, "Young man, your sins are forgiven!"

The people were shocked. "Only God can forgive sins," they said. "That's what the Temple is there for!"

"All right, then," said Jesus. "Supposing I say, 'Get up, pick up your stretcher, and walk'? Perhaps that'll show you that this Son of Man has God's authority to forgive sins!"

The people looked at Jesus and shook their heads, but then something wonderful happened. The paralyzed man did just what Jesus had told him. He got up, picked up his stretcher, and walked. The people were stunned. They looked at Jesus, who was smiling, and then everyone cheered and praised God.

# What is the Sabbath For?

Where's this in the Bible?

Matthew 12

The Judean people took care every week to stop work and rest on the seventh day. This special day, called the "Sabbath", was a sign that one day God would give the world a great holiday. It would be a wonderful celebration, lasting forever. God would rule the world with his love and healing power. But Jesus knew that God's rule was already beginning. So he often chose to heal people on the Sabbath.

One Sabbath day, Jesus was walking with his disciples near a cornfield. The disciples were hungry, and they began to eat a few bits of the grain. Some experts in the Law of Moses noticed them doing this, and they said to Jesus, "Look here! Your disciples are doing something that's not allowed on the Sabbath!"

Calmly, Jesus turned to them, and said: "Did you never read in the Bible about what David did when he and his men were hungry? They went into God's Temple and ate the holy bread, which only the priests were allowed to eat. But now I tell you that someone greater than the Temple is here!" Then Jesus looked around at everyone and declared, "The Sabbath was made for humans, not humans for the Sabbath. So this Son of Man is in charge of the Sabbath!"

That made some of the people angry, especially the leaders who were experts in the Law of Moses. They didn't like the way Jesus was upsetting their way of life.

What else in God's big story links up with this?

**Jubilee!**
p. 52

# Jesus Teaches People about God

Where's this in the Bible?

Matthew 5–7

Jesus took his disciples up into the hills and there he taught them about God's kingdom. This is how he began:

"Blessings on you who are poor in spirit! The kingdom of God will be yours.
Blessings on you who mourn! You will be comforted.
Blessings on you who are humble and lowly! The earth will be yours.
Blessings on you who hunger and thirst for God's justice! You will be satisfied.
Blessings on you who are kind and merciful! Kindness and mercy will be yours.
Blessings on you who are pure in heart! You will see God.
Blessings on you peacemakers! You are the children of God."

Jesus taught his followers that God loves everyone, and his people should love everyone as well. That means forgiving people, just as God longs to forgive us. God wants people to talk to him as they would talk to a loving father. And they should trust God for everything.

Jesus also taught them how to pray. This is the prayer he gave them:

"Father in heaven, may your name be honoured, may your kingdom come, may your will be done on earth as in heaven. Give us the bread we need for today, and forgive us the wrongs we have done, as we forgive people who have wronged us. Don't let us fall into temptation, but rescue us from evil."

Jesus ended his teaching with a warning. Following his teaching, he said, would be like building a house on rock. Doing anything else would be like building a house on sand. The wind and the rain would knock it down and wash it away.

What else in God's big story links up with this?

**On God's Mountain**
p. 44

**God is Love**
p. 274

# Jesus Heals a Girl

Where's this
in the Bible?

Matthew 9

One day, Jesus was teaching a large crowd of people when a man ran up and interrupted him. The man's name was Jairus. He was a leader in the local synagogue. "Please, please!" he begged. "Come and heal my girl! She's going to die!"

Jesus went with him, and the crowd followed. On the way, a woman who was very ill crept through the crowd until she was close to Jesus. Then, she stretched out her hand and touched his clothes. At once she knew she'd been healed.

Jesus knew it too. "Who touched me?" he asked. With tears of joy in her eyes, the woman looked at Jesus and explained what she had done. Jesus smiled at her. "It's your faith!" he said. "That's why you've been healed."

As they were approaching Jairus' house, some people came out to meet him. They too had tears in their eyes, but these were tears of sorrow. "It's too late," they said to Jairus. "Your daughter has just died."

Jairus looked at Jesus. "Don't be afraid," said Jesus. "Just believe!" By now the house was full of people crying and wailing. "She isn't dead," Jesus told them. "She's asleep." But they just laughed at him. Then, while the crowd waited outside, Jesus went into the house, along with the girl's parents and three of his disciples. Quietly, they went into the room where the girl was lying, completely still.

Jesus gently took her hand, and whispered, "Time to get up." And straight away the girl got up. Jesus told her parents to give her something to eat. He also told them not to tell anyone what had happened.

What else in God's big story
links up with this?

**The Man Who Came
Back to Life**
p. 192

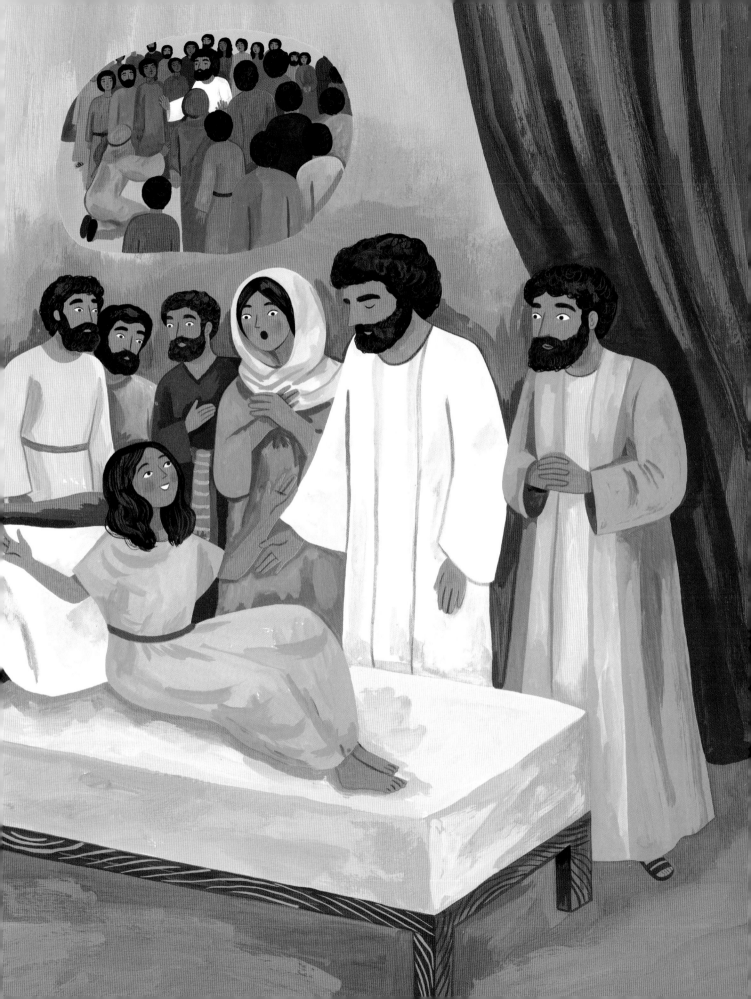

# The Farmer Sows the Seed

Where's this in the Bible?

Matthew 13

Jesus wanted to explain to people how God's kingdom was at last arriving. Long ago, the prophets had promised that one day there would be a new sort of harvest. God would sow new seed, and God's people would grow strong and healthy again, with new faith.

So Jesus told the people this story:

"A farmer went out to sow some seeds. As he scattered the seeds, some of them fell on the path. The birds flew down and gobbled them up. Some of the seeds fell on rocky ground. These seeds started to grow into plants, but they couldn't take root, so they shrivelled up and died. Some seeds landed where there were thorns and thistles. When the plants started to grow, the thorns and thistles grew up around them and choked them. But some seeds fell on good soil, and grew into strong, healthy plants. The plants produced lots of good fruit, and then there was a great harvest."

Jesus looked at the puzzled faces of the people around him. He was teasing them, getting them to think what the story meant. "If you've got ears," he said, "then listen carefully!"

Jesus was telling them that God was starting to do what he had promised long ago. But not everyone was going to be happy with it. Only if people listened carefully and saw what God was doing through Jesus would they become like the strong, healthy plants producing good fruit.

What else in God's big story links up with this?

**The Promise of a New World**
p. 132

# The Woman at the Well

Where's this in the Bible?

John 4

Jesus and his disciples were on a long journey, travelling from Judea in the south to Galilee in the north. On their way they had to go through the land of Samaria, where they decided to stop for a rest. It was around midday, and the sun was hot. The disciples went to find some food in a nearby town, while Jesus stayed back and sat down by a well. After a while, a woman came from the town to fetch water.

To her surprise Jesus asked her for a drink. "You know," he said, "you could have asked me, and I would have given you fresh, living water."

"But sir," replied the woman, "you haven't got a bucket." Jesus replied, "Anyone who drinks this well water will soon be thirsty again. But anyone who drinks the water I'll give them won't ever be thirsty again." When she heard that, the woman said, "Sir, give me this water!"

"Call your husband," said Jesus. "I haven't got a husband," she replied. "Quite right," answered Jesus. "You've had five of them, and the one you now have isn't your husband!" Then the woman's eyes narrowed. "You're a Judean, aren't you?" she said. "You worship in Jerusalem, but we Samaritans worship here."

"Ah," said Jesus, "but God is looking for people to worship him in spirit and truth."

"Oh well," said the woman. "When God's true king comes, he'll explain all that."

Jesus looked at her intently and said, "That's who I am." At that, the woman dropped the jar of water she was holding and dashed off to the town to tell people she had met God's king. Soon after, Jesus' disciples came back. "Look," said Jesus. "It's harvest-time! People are ready for the message!"

What else in God's big story links up with this?

**Water from a Rock**
p. 42

# Jesus Feeds a Big Crowd

Where's this in the Bible?

Matthew 14, John 6

Sometimes Jesus would go away from the towns and villages into the desert, and large crowds would follow him. He would teach them many things, explaining about God's kingdom.

Once, after Jesus had been teaching all day, his disciples saw that it was getting late and realized nobody had eaten anything. They told Jesus he should send the crowds away so they could go home and find some food.

"They don't need to go away," replied Jesus. "You can give them some food here." The disciples were puzzled. There were about 5,000 men along with their wives and children.

"What do you mean?" they said. "Where can we get enough food for all these people?"

Then one of the disciples told Jesus he'd found a boy who had with him five loaves of bread and two fish, but obviously that wouldn't be enough for everyone.

Jesus told all the people to sit down. He asked the boy to give him the loaves and the fish. Then he looked up to heaven and blessed the food. He broke the bread and gave it to his disciples, and his disciples gave it to the crowd. Then they did the same with the fish. And everyone had enough to eat!

When they had all finished eating, Jesus told his disciples to pick up the bits that were left over, and they collected 12 baskets full of bread and fish.

All the people who saw it were amazed. "This must surely be the prophet God promised to send us," they said.

What else in God's big story links up with this?

**Water from a Rock**
p. 42

# Jesus and the Big Storm

Where's this in the Bible?

Matthew 14

After the big crowd had been fed, the people wanted to make Jesus their king. But he sent them away and went off into the hills on his own to pray to God.

Meanwhile, some of the disciples boarded a boat and were crossing over the Sea of Galilee to Capernaum. It was late at night, and when they were near the middle of the sea a fierce storm suddenly blew up. It was very frightening. The waves were smashing into the boat, and the wind was stopping it from getting any further.

Then, at the dead of night, they saw a figure walking toward them on the water! It was Jesus, but they thought it must be a ghost. They were terrified, and they screamed for help.

But Jesus spoke to them in a kind voice. "Cheer up!" he said. "It's me! Don't be afraid."

"If it's really you," yelled Peter, "tell me to come over to you on the water!"

"All right," said Jesus, "come on, then!" Peter got out of the boat and started to walk on the water toward Jesus. But when he saw the wind and the waves he was afraid, and he began to sink. "Master!" he yelled. "Rescue me!"

Jesus reached out his hand and caught him. "Not much faith there!" he said. "Why did you stop believing?"

Jesus and Peter got into the boat, and the wind died down. Everyone was amazed. "You really are God's Son!" they said.

What else in God's big story links up with this?

**Trusting in God**
p. 272

THE NEW TESTAMENT

# Who Do You Think I Am?

Where's this in the Bible?

Matthew 16

Jesus decided to take his group of 12 disciples to a place in the north, far away from all the crowds. When they got there, Jesus asked his disciples what people were saying about him.

"They're saying you're a prophet," they replied. "Some people say you're John the Baptist. Others say you're another Elijah. Or Jeremiah."

"But what about you?" asked Jesus. "Who do you think I am?"

Peter answered, "You are God's Son. You are God's true king!" Jesus turned to Peter and blessed him. Then he said, "You are Peter, the rock, and on this rock I will build my church."

Then Jesus warned them that things were going to get tough. They had to go to Jerusalem, where he, Jesus, would be arrested, beaten, and killed. But afterward he would be raised from the dead.

Peter was cross. "No!" he said. "That can't happen!"

But then Jesus was cross with Peter. "You mustn't try to get in my way," he said. "You're thinking like people think, not like God thinks!"

Then Jesus told his disciples that if they wanted to be with him they would have to be willing to suffer, just like him. But if they stayed loyal to him they would see that God's kingdom was at last arriving.

What else in God's big story links up with this?

**Who Should Be King?**
p. 74

# Transfiguration!

One day, Jesus asked his three closest disciples, Peter, James, and John, to go with him up a high mountain. They were all alone at the top of the mountain praying when, suddenly, Jesus looked totally different. His face shone like the sun! His clothes became dazzling white, too.

Peter, James, and John were stunned. They fell down in amazement and fear.

Then, just as suddenly, they saw two other men standing either side of Jesus. One of the men was Moses and the other was Elijah. They were talking to Jesus about what would happen to him in Jerusalem. And both of them were shining like Jesus.

Peter was so excited he couldn't help saying something. "This is wonderful!" he said. "Let's make three shelters: one for you, one for Moses, and one for Elijah!"

But then a bright cloud came down and surrounded them. A voice came out of the cloud.

"This is my Son," said the voice, "and I'm delighted with him. Listen carefully to all he says!"

When Peter, James, and John heard the voice, they were scared out of their wits! But then Jesus came over to them and touched them. "Don't be afraid," he said. "Get up! We must be going. But you must promise not to tell anyone what you saw until this Son of Man has been raised from the dead."

Where's this in the Bible?

Mark 9,
Luke 9

What else in God's big story links up with this?

**On God's Mountain**
p. 44

**Elijah and the Prophets of Baal**
p. 100

# Heading for Jerusalem

Where's this in the Bible?

Luke 9

Jesus told his disciples it was time to go to Jerusalem. "Listen carefully!" he said. "We're going to Jerusalem, and when we're there this Son of Man will be arrested and condemned to death. But on the third day he will be raised back to life."

The road to Jerusalem took them through Samaria, and they decided to stop in one of the villages. But the people there didn't want Jesus coming through their region. At this, James and John got very angry. "Why don't we call for fire to come down from heaven and burn them up?" they asked.

Jesus was cross with James and John. He hadn't come to burn people up! So they went to another village and continued their journey. Along the way, several people said they wanted to go with Jesus. Jesus warned them that it would be difficult.

One person said, "I will follow you wherever you go!"

Jesus replied, "Foxes have their lairs, and birds have their nests, but this Son of Man doesn't have anywhere to call his home."

Another person wanted to wait until his father had died before following Jesus. "No," said Jesus, "you have to come right now. Now is the time to announce God's kingdom!"

Another person wanted to go home first and say goodbye to their family. "No," said Jesus, "If you begin ploughing a field and then start looking back over your shoulder, the plough won't go straight. You have to keep your eyes fixed on what's ahead if you want to be part of God's kingdom."

# The Kind Foreigner

Where's this in the Bible?

Luke 10

When Jesus was teaching the people, sometimes a person would ask him a question. One day a man who was an expert in the Law of Moses thought he would put Jesus on the spot.

The man asked Jesus, "What must I do to be part of God's new world?" Jesus replied by asking a question in return. "What does the Law teach?" he asked. The man answered straight away. "You must love God and love your neighbour," he said.

"That's right!" said Jesus. "Ah yes," said the expert, "but who is my neighbour?"

Jesus answered him with this story:

"Once a man was travelling from Jerusalem to Jericho, when he was attacked by robbers. They took all his money and left him at the side of the road, half dead. A priest came past. He saw the man but he carried on with his journey. Then a Temple servant came past. He saw the man but he carried on with his journey too. Next, a foreigner from Samaria came past, and as soon as he saw the man he took pity on him. Carefully, the Samaritan cleaned and bandaged the man's wounds, then he lifted him onto his donkey and took him to an inn. He even left some money to pay for the man to stay there until he recovered."

Jesus looked the expert in the eye. "Now," he said, "which of the three was the 'neighbour' of the man who'd been attacked?"

"I suppose," said the expert, "the one who helped him."

"That's right!" said Jesus. "Now, you go and do the same."

What else in God's big story links up with this?

**Jesus Teaches People about God**
p. 162

# Jesus Visits Two Sisters

Where's this in the Bible?

Luke 10

When Jesus was in Judea, he often visited a family who lived in Bethany, a village near Jerusalem. There were two sisters, Martha and Mary, and their brother, Lazarus. Martha was the one who ran the household.

One day, Jesus was in the front room talking with his disciples when Mary came in and sat with them. She was eager to hear Jesus' teaching.

Martha was on her own at the back of the house in the kitchen. She was working hard trying to get everything done, when suddenly she stopped and looked around. "Where's that sister of mine?" she said to herself. "She's never here when I need her!"

Martha went into the front room, where she found Mary listening to Jesus. "Master," Martha said, "don't you care that my sister has left me to do all the work by myself? Tell her she needs to help!"

"Martha, Martha," replied Jesus in a kind voice, "you're getting stressed and distracted about so many things. But there's just one thing that really matters. Mary has chosen what matters most, and it will not be taken away from her."

# Jesus Blesses the Children

Where's this in the Bible?

Matthew 18, 19

Once, Jesus' disciples were arguing about which of them was the most important. So Jesus took a little child by the hand and brought the child into the middle of the gathering. He smiled at the child and said to his disciples, "Unless you become humble, like this little child, you will never enter God's kingdom.

"What's more," he added, "anyone who welcomes a little child in my name, welcomes me. And anyone who welcomes me, welcomes the one who sent me."

Another time, parents were bringing their children to Jesus and asking him to say a prayer of blessing for them. But Jesus' disciples didn't want that. They thought Jesus should be allowed to carry on teaching the crowds, and not be bothered by children.

Jesus told his disciples they were wrong. "Let the little children come to me," he said. "Don't stop them! God's kingdom belongs to people like them! In fact, you must all welcome God as king in your lives, just like a child does. That's the only way you can belong to him."

And he hugged the children, placed his hands on their heads, and said prayers of blessing for them.

# The Father Who Forgave

Where's this in the Bible?

Luke 15

Jesus was having a party. Lots of people came, including some who had done bad things. Some experts in the Law of Moses noticed this and got very cross. "This man, Jesus," they said, "who does he think he is? Eating and drinking with all these sinners!" So Jesus told them this story:

"Once there was a man who had two sons. The younger son asked his father for his share of the family savings. He travelled a long way from home and made friends in another land, where he spent all the money on wild and selfish living. Then, when all the money was gone, there was a famine in the land, and all the friends he'd made simply disappeared. As he had no money, the young man had to find work. But the only work he could find was looking after pigs. He was so hungry he felt he could eat anything, even the horrible food the pigs were eating!

"One day, the young man came to his senses. He thought, 'My father's servants live better than this. I will go and say sorry and offer to be his servant.' So he set off. While he was still some distance away, his father saw him. He ran to his son and hugged him tightly. Next, he called for his servants to bring his son fine clothes, new shoes, and a ring, then told them to prepare a great feast to celebrate his son's return.

"But when the older brother came home from his work, he was angry. 'What's my brother done to deserve all this?' he asked. 'What about me?' The father replied, 'My son, you are always with me. All that I have is yours. But we have to celebrate! Your brother was dead, and now he's alive. He was lost, and now he's found.'"

Jesus told this story to show that when he was celebrating with people who were sorry for the bad things they had done, this was part of God's great plan to put everything right.

What else in God's big story links up with this?

**God Promises to Rescue His People**
p. 118

**Paul Explains God's Plan**
p. 260

THE NEW TESTAMENT

# The Good Shepherd

Where's this in the Bible?

John 10

Jesus wanted the people to trust him. He knew that God had sent him to be their leader, and he needed to warn them that other leaders shouldn't be trusted.

"I am the real shepherd," he said. "I'm the one the sheep have been waiting for. Others may try to lead, but they will only lead the sheep into trouble. I have come to give you life. Full, overflowing life!

"I am the good shepherd," he went on. "I will do anything for my sheep. I will even give my life for them. I know my sheep and my sheep know me, just like I know my Father and my Father knows me.

"I have other sheep, too," said Jesus. "They come from lots of different places. But I will call them, and they also will hear my voice. Then there will be one flock, and one shepherd."

People were puzzled. What did Jesus mean? Was he really the leader that God's people were waiting for?

"Look at what I've been doing!" said Jesus. "That will show you who I am. I am calling my sheep, and they will hear my voice. I will keep them safe forever, and I will give them life in God's new world."

What else in God's big story links up with this?

**Yahweh is My Shepherd**
p. 78

**Trusting in God**
p. 272

# The Man in the Tree

Where's this in the Bible?

Luke 19

Jesus and his disciples were getting nearer to Jerusalem. They had reached the town of Jericho. In Jericho, there lived a man called Zacchaeus. Nobody liked him because he'd made himself very rich by working for the Romans.

Zacchaeus wasn't very tall. He couldn't see over people's heads. But he wanted to see Jesus. So he climbed up a tree!

As Jesus walked by with his disciples, Jesus looked up and saw Zacchaeus peering through the branches.

"Come down, Zacchaeus!" said Jesus. "I'd like to share a meal with you today!" Zacchaeus was so surprised that he nearly fell out of the tree. Quickly he climbed down and welcomed Jesus into his house.

People were shocked. "It's a disgrace!" said some of them, while others muttered, "He's going to eat with a sinner!"

But Zacchaeus stood there and declared, "Master, I'm going to change. I'm giving away half my property to the poor. And if there's anyone I've cheated, I'm going to pay them back four times over!"

Jesus looked around and smiled. "God has come to the rescue, right here!" he said. "Zacchaeus is a true son of Abraham. This Son of Man is here to seek out people lost in sin, like him, and rescue them."

What else in God's big story links up with this?

**The Father Who Forgave**
p. 186

# The Man Who Came Back to Life

Where's this in the Bible?

John 11

One day, Jesus received a message from his two friends Mary and Martha. "Come quickly," the message said. "Lazarus, our brother, is very ill." But Jesus stayed where he was for two days. On the third day he told his disciples they had to leave, but they said they didn't want to go back near Jerusalem. Then Jesus told them what had happened. "Our friend Lazarus has fallen asleep," he said, "and I'm going to wake him up."

"Master," replied his disciples, "if he's asleep, he'll be all right." Then Jesus spoke to them plainly. "Lazarus," he said, "is dead. Come on, let's go."

When they were near the house, Martha ran out to greet Jesus. "Master," she said, "if you had been here, my brother wouldn't have died."

Jesus wanted to comfort Martha. "Lazarus will rise again," he said. Martha sighed. "I know he will rise again in the future," she said, "on the last day, when everyone is raised from the dead." Then Jesus declared, "I am the resurrection and the life!"

Jesus came to Lazarus's tomb, followed by a crowd of mourners. There was a large stone across the entrance. Everyone was crying. Then Jesus burst into tears as well. "Take the stone away," he said. "But he's been dead four days!" cried Martha. "There'll be a bad smell!" Jesus tried to calm her. "If you believe," he said, "you will see God's glory."

They rolled away the stone, and Jesus prayed, "Thank you, Father, for listening to me." Then he shouted: "Lazarus! Come out!" And out came Lazarus, wrapped in the strips of cloth in which they had buried him. "Unwrap him," said Jesus, "and let him go."

What else in God's big story links up with this?

**Jesus Heals a Girl**
p. 164

**Jesus Rises from the Dead**
p. 220

# Mary Anoints Jesus' Feet

Where's this
in the Bible?

John 12

Once, when Jesus was at Bethany, he and his disciples were sharing a meal at the house of Mary, Martha, and Lazarus. Martha, as usual, was doing the cooking, but Mary had something else in mind.

She went to her room and fetched a large jar of sweet-smelling ointment. Then she came and knelt in front of Jesus. She opened the jar and poured the ointment onto his feet. The room went quiet, and everyone watched as Mary began to wipe Jesus' feet with her hair. The whole house was filled with the lovely scent of the ointment.

Suddenly, the silence was broken by an angry voice. One of Jesus' disciples stood up and pointed an accusing finger at Mary. His name was Judas Iscariot. "You could have sold that ointment for a lot of money," he said, "and then given the money to the poor."

Jesus looked at Judas. "Don't be angry with her," he said calmly. "She was keeping the ointment for me, for when I die and will be buried.

"After all," he went on, "you will always have poor people with you. But you won't always have me."

# Jesus Enters Jerusalem

Where's this in the Bible?

Matthew 21; Luke 19

Jesus decided it was time to go to Jerusalem. He knew that a long time ago, one of God's prophets had said to the Judeans: "Here comes your king, riding on a donkey!" So he asked his disciples to fetch him a donkey. When people saw Jesus riding on the donkey, some of them spread their cloaks on the road in front of him. Others took small branches from the trees and scattered them on the road. Some of the crowd went on ahead, dancing, singing, and clapping their hands, while those behind shouted out:

"Hosanna now to David's Son!
God's blessing on the coming one,
The one who comes in the Lord's own name!
Hosanna in the highest!"

Soon the whole city was gripped with excitement. Even little children joined in the song, which annoyed some of the city rulers. "Tell those children to be quiet!" they said.

But Jesus sprang to their defence. "Even if they were silent," he said, "these stones here would start singing! Don't you know what the Bible says? 'Special praise comes from small people.'"

Jesus was riding toward Jerusalem down a steep hill called the Mount of Olives. He could see the Temple, straight ahead in the distance, and his eyes filled with tears. Turning to the crowd, he cried: "If only you had known that God was coming back to give you peace. But you've refused to listen. Now it's too late! The days are coming when your enemies will bring you crashing to the ground."

What else in God's big story links up with this?

**When Will God Return?**
p. 124

# Jesus and the Temple

Where's this in the Bible?

Matthew 21, John 2

It was Passover time. When Jesus reached the Temple courtyards, he saw lots of people who had travelled there for the festival.

Many people wanted to buy animals for sacrifice, but you could only use the special Temple coins. Jesus could see that the traders who were changing the money, and those who were selling the animals, were charging far too much. That made Jesus angry. So he drove the traders and the animals out of the courtyard. He tipped over the traders' tables, and the coins scattered everywhere, clattering over the cobblestones. "Take these things away!" he told the traders. "You're turning my Father's house into a market!"

The Temple guards heard the commotion and ran to find out what was happening. When they saw Jesus, they started to question him. "Why are you doing this?" they asked. Jesus answered by saying, "If you destroy this Temple, I'll build it again in three days!"

They looked at him and frowned. "What are you talking about?" they said. "It's taken nearly 50 years to build this Temple!" But Jesus didn't mean he would build a temple made of stone. Jesus' disciples were puzzled too. Only later did they begin to understand.

Some of the Temple rulers went up to Jesus and asked, "By what authority are you doing these things?" Jesus replied with a question. "Remember John the Baptist? Where did his authority come from? Was it from God? Or not?" (Jesus asked this because John had said that Jesus was God's true king, and everybody knew that the king would take charge of the Temple.) The Temple rulers didn't have an answer. They didn't want to say "Yes". But they were afraid to say "No", because the people would be angry. For they all believed that John was a great prophet.

What else in God's big story links up with this?

**The Wonderful Temple**
p. 92

**New Temple, New Thinking**
p. 256

# Death in the Vineyard

Where's this in the Bible?

Matthew 21

Jesus wanted to explain to the Temple rulers what God was doing, so he told them this story:

"There was once a man who owned a vineyard. The man had to go away, so he let the vineyard out to some farmers and told them to look after it carefully. After a while the owner of the vineyard sent a servant to ask for the fruit. But the farmers beat him up and sent him away. The owner of the vineyard sent another servant, then another, and another, but the same thing happened each time.

"Then he said, 'This time I'll send my beloved son. Surely they will respect him.' But when they saw the son the farmers said, 'Let's kill him, and then we can have the vineyard for ourselves!' And that's what they did."

Jesus looked at the Temple rulers. "So," he said, "what do you think the owner of the vineyard will do next?" The answer was obvious. "He will get rid of those greedy and violent farmers," they said, "and give the vineyard to someone else."

"That's right," said Jesus. "Remember what the Bible says about the stones used to build God's Temple: 'The stone that didn't fit the wall will now be placed on top of it all.' In other words, God's kingdom will be taken away from you and be given to people who will produce the fruit."

When the Temple rulers heard this, they realized that the story Jesus had just told was about them. They were the greedy and violent farmers! The Temple rulers wanted to arrest Jesus, but they were afraid of the people, who looked up to him as a prophet.

THE NEW TESTAMENT

What else in God's big story links up with this?

**The Suffering Servant**
p. 120

**In the Garden of Gethsemane**
p. 208

# Whose Head is This?

Where's this
in the Bible?

Matthew 22

Everyone in Judea knew you were supposed to pay taxes to Caesar, the Roman emperor.

But nobody wanted to. It wasn't just because of the money, but because they didn't want Caesar to be their king anyway.

The problem was, if you refused to pay the tax then the Romans would be angry and you would be punished. So, some of the Judean leaders thought they would ask Jesus a trick question.

"We know you speak the truth," they said. "You aren't afraid of anybody. You only teach what God wants. So: should we pay taxes to Caesar, or not?"

Jesus knew it was a trick. "Show me the coin for the tax," he said. They brought him the coin. It had an image of Caesar, and around the edge some words were inscribed that said, "Son of God . . . High Priest."

"This image and this inscription," said Jesus. "Who do they belong to?" "Caesar," they said.

"Well then," said Jesus, "you'd better pay Caesar back what he deserves. And pay God back what he deserves!"

The Judean leaders didn't know what to say. They had thought that this time they'd got Jesus in a corner. Surely, they thought, he will either say something that will get him into trouble with the Romans, or he'll say something that will upset the people. But no matter how hard they tried, they couldn't catch Jesus out.

# Jesus' Last Meal with His Disciples

Where's this in the Bible?

Matthew 26

It was Passover time. Families and friends were gathering for the festival. They told one another the story of how God had rescued their ancestors from slavery in Egypt. It reminded them that God had promised he would rescue them again.

Jesus and his disciples got together for the Passover meal. Jesus said the special prayers and they talked about how God had rescued his people. Then Jesus did something that surprised them. He took some bread, and broke it into pieces. Then he gave it to them and said, "Take this and eat it. This is my body, broken for you."

Then he poured out some wine, and passed round the cup. "This is my blood," he said. "God is making a new special agreement with you, and with many others. After I've gone away, you must go on sharing bread and wine together. It will remind you of me and all that I've done for you. It will remind you that this is how God is offering you forgiveness!"

Then Jesus became very sad. "One of you," he said, "is going to betray me and hand me over to the Temple rulers."

Nobody knew who Jesus meant, except one of them. His name was Judas Iscariot.

What else in God's big story links up with this?

**The First Passover**
p. 38

# Jesus Washes His Disciples' Feet

Where's this in the Bible?

John 13

While they were together for the Passover, Jesus did something else that surprised his disciples. He took off his cloak, and then got a towel and wrapped it around his waist. Then he took a bowl of water and began to wash his disciples' feet. They were all shocked by this. Washing someone's feet was normally something only a slave would do.

When it came to Peter's turn he stood up and said, "Master, you can't do this! I won't let you wash my feet!"

"Well," said Jesus, "if I don't wash you, you don't belong to my people."

"In that case," said Peter, "don't just wash my feet, wash my hands and my head, too!"

"All you need, actually," smiled Jesus, "is for me to wash your feet. The rest of you is already clean."

When he had finished, Jesus put his cloak back on. "What I did for you just now," he said, "is what you must do for one another."

Then Jesus looked sadly at Peter and said, "Peter, you need to watch out! Before morning, when the rooster crows, you will have told people that you don't even know me."

Peter looked hurt. "Even if I have to die with you," he said, "I won't ever disown you!" And all the others said the same.

# In the Garden of Gethsemane

Where's this in the Bible?

Matthew 26

When they had finished the Passover meal, Jesus and his disciples went outside. They walked up the Mount of Olives until they came to a quiet place called the Garden of Gethsemane, where they stopped to rest. It was getting late, and they were all feeling sleepy after their meal, but Jesus asked Peter, James, and John to stay awake with him. Then he walked on a little way on his own and knelt down to pray.

"Father," he said, "this cup of suffering. Please, please don't make me drink it! But what matters is what you want, not what I want."

Peter and the others were drifting off to sleep. Jesus came and warned them. "Watch out!" he said. "The time of trouble is about to happen."

Jesus went off and knelt down again to pray. He was in agony. He knew that something terrible was about to happen, and he knew he had to go through with it, but it was still terrifying.

He came back to his disciples again, and this time he found them fast asleep. "Wake up!" he said. "Pray that you won't have to face the time of trouble."

Then suddenly a group of Temple guards appeared. At the front, leading the way, was Judas Iscariot.

Peter drew a sword and tried to fight them off. But Jesus stopped him. "People who use the sword," he said, "will die by the sword."

Then the guards took hold of Jesus and marched him away.

What else in God's big story links up with this?

**Death in the Vineyard**
p. 200

# Jesus is Put on Trial

Where's this in the Bible?

Matthew 26–27; John 18, 19

The Temple guards took Jesus to the high priest. He was the leader of a council made up of priests, experts in the Law of Moses and other officials. Most of them thought Jesus was a troublemaker, teaching people dangerous ideas. They wanted to get rid of him.

"What's this we hear about destroying the Temple and building it again?" they said. Jesus didn't reply. "All right, then," said the high priest, "so are you the true king, God's own Son?"

Jesus looked him in the eye and answered in a calm voice, "You've said the words; and you will see this Son of Man sitting at God's right hand, raised up to God on the clouds of heaven."

"You can't say that!" they all shouted. "It's an offence against God!" And the council decided that Jesus deserved to die.

In the morning the Temple guards took Jesus to Pilate, the Roman governor of Judea. "We found this man making trouble!" they said.

Pilate turned to Jesus. "So," he said, "are you king of the Judeans?" Jesus replied, "I've come to tell people the truth." Pilate threw his head back and laughed. "Truth!" he snorted. "What's that?"

Every year at Passover, Pilate would release one prisoner as a way of pleasing the crowds.

"Shall I release your king?" he asked the crowd. "No!" they shouted. "The only king we have is Caesar! Release Barabbas instead!" Barabbas was a convicted robber and a murderer.

In the end, Pilate gave in. He let the murderer go free and condemned Jesus to death.

What else in God's big story links up with this?

**Daniel and the Monsters**
p. 116

# Peter Denies Knowing Jesus

Where's this in the Bible?

Matthew 26; Luke 22

When Jesus was arrested in the Garden of Gethsemane, all his disciples ran away. But Peter secretly followed Jesus to the high priest's house.

Peter joined some people in the courtyard just outside. They were warming themselves by a fire. After a while, a servant girl noticed Peter and said, "Aren't you one of Jesus' friends?"

Peter looked alarmed. "No!" he answered. "Certainly not!"

Later, another servant saw him and said to the others, "I'm sure I've seen him with Jesus!"

"No!" said Peter. "I don't know the man."

Then one of the others said, "You're from Galilee, like Jesus, aren't you? We can tell by the way you talk."

At that, Peter began to curse. "No, you're all wrong!" he shouted. "I don't know him. You're confusing me with someone else!"

Inside the high priest's house, Jesus turned and looked at Peter. And at that moment, Peter heard the sound of a rooster crowing. Then he remembered what Jesus had said to him: "Before morning, when the rooster crows, you will have told people that you don't even know me."

Peter suddenly felt so ashamed. How could he have said those things? He stumbled away, his head in his hands, and broke down in tears.

What else in God's big story links up with this?

**Breakfast on the Shore**
p. 226

THE NEW TESTAMENT

# The Journey to the Cross

Where's this in the Bible?

Matthew 27; Luke 22–23

Jesus had been condemned to death by Pilate, the Roman governor, and was being guarded by Roman soldiers. The soldiers whipped him and beat him. They blindfolded him and teased him, challenging him to guess who was hitting him. Then they pretended to worship him. They made a crown out of thorns and pushed it down on his head. "All hail, king of the Judeans!" they shouted.

When they had finished mocking Jesus, the soldiers forced him to carry a big plank of wood that was going to be made into his cross. They made him carry it through the streets and up a steep hill outside the city, where criminals were taken to die. A crowd gathered to watch. The load was too heavy, and Jesus kept stumbling under its weight. So some soldiers went into the crowd, grabbed a man called Simon, and made him carry the cross instead.

While Jesus was being marched along, he could hear some women in the crowd calling his name and weeping. "Don't cry for me," he said. "Cry for yourselves and your children. If they do this to me, think what they'll do to real troublemakers!"

At last, they reached the top of a hill where Jesus knew he would die. It was called Golgotha, which means "the place of a skull". There the soldiers made Jesus lie down on the cross while they hammered nails through his hands and feet and into the wood.

"Forgive them, Father," prayed Jesus. "They don't know what they're doing!"

Pilate had ordered the soldiers to put a notice up on top of the cross, over Jesus' head. It was written in Hebrew, Greek, and Latin. The notice said: "Jesus of Nazareth, king of the Judeans."

# Jesus is Crucified

Where's this in the Bible?

Matthew 27;
Luke 23;
John 19

The soldiers lifted the cross Jesus was lying on and stood it upright in the ground. This was how the Romans punished criminals who they thought were dangerous and causing trouble. They called the punishment "crucifixion". It meant a slow, agonizing death for those who were crucified. The soldiers took Jesus' cloak and decided to gamble to see who would have it.

It was about nine o'clock in the morning. As Jesus was hanging on the cross, people came up to watch and to laugh at him. Some of them jeered, "So! You were going to pull down the Temple and build it again in three days? You'd better start by coming down from that cross!"

Some of the Temple rulers and experts in the Law of Moses came to watch, too. "Look at you!" they said. "You rescued other people, but you can't rescue yourself! If you're the king of the Judeans, why don't you come down from the cross? Then we'll believe you!"

They crucified two robbers with Jesus, one on either side of him. One of them joined in with those who were mocking Jesus, but the other one stopped him. "No!" he said. "We're getting what we deserve, but this man has done nothing wrong." Then he turned to Jesus. "Jesus!" he said. "When you become king, remember me!" Jesus turned his head to him and said, "This very day, you and I will be in Paradise together."

Jesus looked down from the cross and saw two people looking up at him, their faces etched in sorrow. One was Mary, his mother, and next to her was a young disciple whom Jesus loved. "Look, mother!" cried Jesus. "There's your son." Then he said to the disciple, "Look, son. There's your mother."

It was now midday, but the sky had become very dark.

What else in God's big story links up with this?

**Sin and Forgiveness**
p. 50

**The Suffering Servant**
p. 120

# Jesus Dies and is Buried

Where's this in the Bible?

Matthew 27;
John 19

At about three o'clock in the afternoon, when it was still dark, Jesus cried out, "My God, my God, why did you abandon me?" Someone thought he was asking for a drink. They filled a sponge with sour wine and held it up to him on the end of a pole. Then Jesus gave another loud cry. "It's all done!" he said. And he bowed his head and died.

At that very moment, the great curtain inside the Temple was torn in two, from top to bottom. A Roman soldier who was watching Jesus shook his head. "This man really was God's Son," he said. Then another soldier took his spear and stuck it into Jesus' body, to check that he was really dead.

Meanwhile, a rich man called Joseph wanted to make sure that Jesus received a proper burial. Joseph had been a follower of Jesus, but he had kept it secret because he knew Jesus had powerful enemies. Now he went to Pilate and asked his permission to bury Jesus' body.

Joseph took Jesus' lifeless body down from the cross and wrapped it in a new linen cloth. He buried Jesus in a tomb in a beautiful garden. The tomb was like a cave, carved from the side of a rock. Joseph carried the body carefully into the tomb. When he came out, he rolled a big stone across the entrance to make sure nobody could get in.

Some women who were followers of Jesus had been watching from a distance. One of them was a close friend who loved Jesus dearly. Her name was Mary Magdalene. She and a few of her friends had followed Joseph, and they saw where Jesus was buried.

What else in God's big story links up with this?

**God's New Agreement**
p. 268

# Jesus Rises from the Dead

*Where's this in the Bible?*

John 20

Early on Sunday morning, Mary Magdalene went back to visit the tomb where Jesus was buried. She was going to put sweet-smelling spices around Jesus' body. But as she was approaching, she saw that the big stone in front of the entrance had already been rolled away! So Mary turned back and ran to tell the disciples.

Two disciples, Peter and John, ran to the tomb. John got there first and peered in. Then Peter came up and went straight inside. He saw the linen cloths lying where Jesus' body had been, and the cloth that had been around his head folded up by itself. Then John went in too. He saw, and straight away he believed. Jesus must be alive again!

Peter and John went away, but Mary stayed near the tomb, crying. After a while, she got up and looked into the tomb. There she saw two angels where Jesus' body had been lying. "Why are you crying?" the angels asked. Mary was so distressed. "They've taken away my master," she said, "and I don't know where they've put him."

The words had hardly left her mouth when, from the corner of her eye, she noticed a man approaching. She thought he must be the man who looked after the garden. "If you've taken him away," she said, "please, tell me where you've put him." But it wasn't the gardener. It was Jesus!

Jesus was smiling. "Mary!" he said. Mary looked up, and her heart started to pound. "Teacher!" she said. And the tears she was crying turned from tears of sorrow to tears of joy. After a while, Jesus said, "Go and tell my disciples that I'm going to go away to be with my Father and your Father." Mary wanted to stay with Jesus, but she did what he said and went to tell his disciples that Jesus was alive.

*What else in God's big story links up with this?*

**God Promises to Rescue His People**
p. 118

**The Promise of a New World**
p. 132

# On the Road to Emmaus

Where's this in the Bible?

Luke 24

That afternoon, two of Jesus' disciples were walking from Jerusalem to a village called Emmaus. They felt so sad. Jesus, their leader, teacher, and dearest friend, was gone. He had been crucified and buried, and they thought they would never see him again. As the two friends were walking along, Jesus himself came up and walked beside them. They greeted him politely, but they didn't recognize him. "Why are you so sad?" he asked. They answered him, "We were with Jesus of Nazareth. We hoped he would rescue God's people. But he was crucified. And that was three days ago." Jesus replied in a comforting voice. "Don't you see?" he said. "In the Bible it explains that God's Son has to suffer before he becomes king of the world."

They came to Emmaus and went indoors. When they had sat down to eat, Jesus took some bread, blessed it, broke it, and started to share it. And as soon as he did that, they recognized him! But then, before they could say anything, he vanished from their sight. The two friends were amazed. "Of course!" they said. "It was Jesus himself! Our hearts were burning with excitement as he talked to us."

Without waiting to finish their meal, the two friends got up and hurried back to Jerusalem. They found the other disciples and told them what had happened. As they were talking, Jesus appeared in the middle of the room. The disciples were alarmed. Were they seeing a ghost? But Jesus showed them the wounds in his hands and his feet where he had been nailed to the cross. Then they gave him something to eat, and that convinced them that it really was Jesus, raised from the dead.

"It's nearly time," said Jesus. "God has new work for you to do, and he will give you his own special power to do it."

What else in God's big story links up with this?

**The Suffering Servant**
p. 120

# The Disciple Who Doubted

Where's this in the Bible?

John 20

One of Jesus' disciples, Thomas, was always asking awkward questions. He hadn't wanted to come to Jerusalem on that last trip, but he loved Jesus enough to go with him anyway. He didn't always understand what Jesus was saying, but he stayed loyal.

Thomas hadn't been with the other disciples when Jesus had appeared in the middle of the room. They told him, over and over, that they had seen Jesus, but he didn't believe them. "I would need to touch him," he said. "I'd need to put my finger into the wounds where the nails went into his hands, and feel where the spear went into his body." He wasn't going to be taken in by their story.

A week later, all the disciples were together in the same house as before. The doors were locked, but suddenly there was Jesus again, standing in the middle of the room.

"All right, Thomas," said Jesus, "bring your finger here and touch my hands. Bring your hand here and feel where the spear went in. Just believe!"

That was enough for Thomas. "My Lord," he said, "and my God!"

Jesus smiled. "All right, Thomas. Now you have seen, and now you have believed. May God bless everyone who believes even though they haven't seen!"

# Breakfast on the Shore

Where's this in the Bible?

John 21

A few days later, some of Jesus' disciples went fishing on the Sea of Galilee. They fished all night but caught nothing. In the morning, while they were still in the boat, Jesus appeared on the shore. But they didn't realize it was him. He called out, "Try casting the net on the right side of the boat!" So that's what they did, and suddenly the net was full of fish! Then they realized it was Jesus. He had made a charcoal fire and was getting ready to cook some breakfast.

When Peter saw it was Jesus, he jumped into the water and swam to shore. They had caught 153 large fish! The net looked as though it would burst. Even so, it didn't break.

After breakfast, Jesus asked Peter, "Do you love me?" And Peter replied, "Yes, you know I'm your friend."

"Then feed my lambs," said Jesus.

Again Jesus asked, "Do you love me?" And again Peter replied, "Yes, you know I'm your friend."

"Then look after my sheep," said Jesus.

A third time, Jesus asked, "Are you my friend?" Peter was sad. "Lord," he said, "you know everything. You know I'm your friend."

"Then feed my sheep," said Jesus.

Jesus told Peter that one day, he would die because of his faith. "But now," said Jesus, "follow me!"

What else in God's big story links up with this?

**Peter Denies Knowing Jesus**
p. 212

**Trusting in God**
p. 272

# Jesus is King!

After God had raised him from the dead, Jesus stayed for 40 days with his disciples, teaching and encouraging them.

They knew from the Bible that God had promised to raise up a true king who would be Lord of all the earth, and who would bring justice and peace to his people.

"When will this happen?" asked the disciples.

Jesus explained that it would happen soon, but not in the way they were expecting. He said he would have to go away, and they would no longer be able to see him. But he would still be with them, helping and guiding them by God's Holy Spirit.

From now on, Jesus would be ruling the world from his new position at God's right hand. Jesus would be in heaven and God's new way of ruling the world would come true on earth.

"This is what will happen," said Jesus. "You will receive the power of God's Spirit. Then you will begin to tell the world all about me. You'll start in Jerusalem, then you'll go to Judea and Samaria, and then on and on to the ends of the earth!"

As Jesus said this, he was lifted up from them, and a cloud took him out of their sight.

Jesus' disciples were excited to know that he was now ruling the world in a whole new way, even though they couldn't see him. They prayed that he would begin to do the wonderful new things he had promised.

What else in God's big story links up with this?

**Praise to the King of Kings!**
p. 134

# Jesus Sends God's Holy Spirit

Where's this in the Bible?

Acts 2

It was now seven weeks since Jesus had risen from the dead. It was also seven weeks since everyone had gathered to celebrate Passover. That meant it was time for another festival: the festival of Pentecost. Every Passover, the Judeans remembered how God had rescued them from Egypt. Every Pentecost, they remembered how God gave Moses his special agreement on Mount Sinai.

This year, Jesus' disciples had gathered in a house in Jerusalem, when suddenly something extraordinary happened. They heard a rushing noise. Louder and louder it got, until it became like a powerful wind, sweeping through the whole house! Then, as the noise died down, there were flames of fire flickering on top of their heads. This was the sign that God's powerful Spirit was coming to live inside them and give them strength for their new work.

All at once, the disciples found that they could speak in different languages! They went outside and began to talk to the crowds. Judeans from all over the world had come to Jerusalem for the festival, and they spoke all sorts of languages. But when the disciples spoke to them, each person could hear what was being said in their own language.

As the disciples were speaking, someone in the crowd started to make fun of them. "Look at them all, babbling away!" they laughed. "They must have had too much to drink!"

But Peter put them right. "We're not drunk!" he said. "This is what the Bible said would happen. God always promised to give people his Spirit. Jesus is God's true king and Lord of the whole world. He has given us his Spirit so that we can tell everyone about him. You need to believe this good news and get baptized, so you can be part of God's people as well."

## What else in God's big story links up with this?

**Jubilee!**
p. 52

**The Wonderful Temple**
p. 92

# The Church is Born

Many people in Jerusalem believed the good news about Jesus. Hundreds were baptized and became his followers. They were eager to hear all that Jesus' disciples were saying about him.

Jesus' new followers began to live together and look after one another as if they were one great big family. It was like having lots of special new brothers and sisters. They even sold their possessions so they could give the money to those who needed it most. At the same time, the disciples healed lots of people who had diseases. It seemed like a whole new world was being born.

Jesus' new followers would gather in peoples' houses to read the Bible and pray together. As Judeans, they had always prayed to God, but now they were able to pray to God through Jesus. They gathered regularly in one another's houses. When they ate together they would break the bread and share it, just as Jesus had told them to. And when they did that, they had the sense that Jesus was right there with them. They called these meetings "assemblies" or "gatherings", which is what we mean when we say "church".

When the rulers in Jerusalem saw what was happening, they didn't like it at all. They were afraid that the people would turn against them, so they tried to make Jesus' disciples stop speaking about him. But Peter stood up and said to them, "We must obey God, not humans!" Then he added, "The God of our ancestors raised Jesus to life after you had had him killed. We are his witnesses – and so is the Holy Spirit, which God has given us."

As they prayed and read the Bible together, all the disciples found that God's Spirit gave them the courage to carry on spreading the good news about Jesus.

# Stephen Tells it Straight

Where's this
in the Bible?

Acts 6–7

More and more people were joining the new "family" of Jesus' followers. But the more the family grew, the more difficult it was to organize. So the disciples chose seven of Jesus' followers to be helpers. They were given the special job of ensuring that everyone was cared for, especially those who were poor. At this time, Peter, James, John, and the other close disciples of Jesus became known as "apostles". Peter and the other apostles placed their hands on the heads of the seven helpers, known as "deacons" and prayed for God's Spirit to guide them.

One of the deacons was Stephen. He was good at explaining how everything God had promised in the Bible was happening at last. He told the Judeans that heaven and earth were coming together through Jesus and the Holy Spirit. But that meant the Temple in Jerusalem would no longer be needed. When they heard that, some of the leaders became angry. They seized Stephen and put him on trial, saying, "This man never stops speaking against God's Temple and the laws that Moses gave us!"

During his trial, Stephen reminded his accusers of what it said in the Bible about God's plan for the world. He explained that Moses and the prophets had looked forward to the time when God would send a leader to be their true king. He showed that in the Bible even the Temple was not as important as they had thought. Then he reminded them that when the true king had appeared among them, they had refused to listen to him. Worse than that, they had betrayed him to the Romans and made sure he was crucified.

That made Stephen's accusers even angrier. They dragged him outside, and stoned him to death. As he died, Stephen had a vision of Jesus standing at God's right hand. "Lord!" he cried. "Don't hold this sin against them!"

What else in God's big story links up with this?

**Daniel and
the Monsters**
p. 116

# Philip Spreads the Word

Where's this in the Bible?

Acts 8

The rulers in Jerusalem had become so angry with Jesus' followers that many of them had to leave the city in case they too were arrested and put on trial. One of them was Philip, who went north to Samaria. He told the people there about Jesus, and lots of them believed and were baptized.

But then an angel spoke to Philip. "Go south to the desert road," he said. So Philip set off, and when he reached the desert road he saw a man in a large chariot, heading south. He was an important official who worked for the queen of Ethiopia. He had been worshipping God in Jerusalem, and now he was on his way back to Africa.

God's Spirit told Philip to run and join the chariot the man was riding in. When he reached the chariot, Philip could see that the man was reading the Bible. He was at the place where the prophet Isaiah says,

"He was led like a sheep to the slaughter,
And as a lamb is silent before its shearers,
So he does not open his mouth . . ."

The man looked up and saw Philip. "Who is the prophet talking about?" asked the man. Philip climbed up into the chariot. He told the man all about Jesus and how he had been killed, like a lamb being sacrificed, and how God had raised him from the dead.

The Ethiopian believed all that Philip said. When they came to some water, they got down from the chariot, and Philip baptized him. Then God's Spirit took Philip away. The Ethiopian went home, full of joy that he now knew Jesus for himself.

What else in God's big story links up with this?

**The Suffering Servant**
p. 120

# On the Road to Damascus

Where's this in the Bible?

Acts 9
1 Corinthians 15

The new family of Jesus' followers was growing bigger every day, and soon people were gathering and forming churches miles away from Judea. But as the churches grew stronger, so did their enemies. One of the fiercest enemies was a young man called Saul. Saul believed that God would send a saviour to rescue his people, but he didn't believe it could be someone who had been crucified. So Saul decided to travel around and hunt down Jesus' followers and put them in prison. He had heard that some of them were in Damascus, a city a long way north of Jerusalem in Syria. He was determined to track them down. Nothing was going to stop him. Or so he thought.

As Saul was approaching the city, a bright, dazzling light suddenly shone down from the sky. He stopped dead in his tracks, and when he looked up he could see Jesus himself looking down at him!

"Saul, Saul," said Jesus, "why are you attacking me? Get up, go into the city, and you will be told what to do."

The light was so bright that Saul was blinded. So the men travelling with him had to lead him into the city. And there, for three days, Saul stayed silent, praying. Soon after, Jesus appeared to Ananias, a Jesus-follower who lived in Damascus. Jesus told Ananias he had to go to Saul. Jesus wanted Saul to start something new. He wanted Saul to tell the whole world that he, Jesus, had overcome the power of evil. Now anyone, anywhere, could be rescued from sin and become part of God's family. Ananias was afraid of Saul, but he obeyed. When he arrived, he put his hands on Saul's eyes and suddenly Saul could see again! Saul was now a changed man. He got up and straight away he asked to be baptized.

THE NEW TESTAMENT

What else in God's big story links up with this?

**Transfiguration!**
p. 176

**John's Vision of Jesus**
p. 276

238

# Peter Has a Vision

Where's this in the Bible?

Acts 10

Around that time, there lived a commander of the Roman army called Cornelius. He was a good man, and always prayed to God. One day, an angel appeared to him and told him to invite Peter to his house.

Meanwhile, Peter also had a vision. In Peter's vision there was a gigantic sheet coming down from heaven, and inside were all sorts of animals. He could hear a voice telling him to get up and eat them, but when Peter saw the animals he was horrified! In the Law of Moses there were rules about which animals people could and couldn't eat. All the animals in his vision were forbidden.

"No!" cried Peter. "I can't do that. I've never eaten anything unholy or unclean!"

But the voice replied, "If God makes something clean, you mustn't call it unclean."

Peter was puzzled. He was trying to work out what the vision could mean, when he heard a knock at the door. Messengers from Cornelius had arrived, inviting him to visit. Peter knew that the Holy Spirit was telling him he had to go with them.

When Peter arrived, Cornelius called his family together and asked Peter to speak to them. Peter explained about the wonderful things that Jesus had done, how he had been killed, and how God had raised him from the dead. Cornelius and his family listened and believed. And then something wonderful happened. God's Holy Spirit came upon them, and Peter suddenly realized what his vision must have meant! He had always believed that people who weren't Judeans were unholy or unclean, like the animals in his vision. But now God was telling him that they could be made clean, through the message about Jesus.

What else in God's big story links up with this?

**An Important Meeting**
p. 246

# God Rescues Peter from Prison

Where's this in the Bible?

Acts 12

Judea had a new king. His name was Herod Agrippa. He thought it would please the people if he attacked the followers of Jesus who lived in Jerusalem. So he arrested one of the apostles, James (the brother of John), and had him killed. Then he arrested Peter and put him in prison, chained to two guards. Agrippa was going to have him killed too.

The other Jesus-followers were scared, but they got together and they prayed that God would help them. That very night, God answered their prayers. Peter had fallen asleep, locked up in prison, when suddenly an angel came and woke him up! Peter's chains fell off, and the doors of the prison opened by themselves. Peter thought he was dreaming. It was only when the angel had led Peter out into the city streets that he realized it was all true. Then the angel disappeared.

Peter went straight to the house where his friends were praying. When he knocked, a maid called Rhoda went to the door. She heard an urgent whisper: "Rhoda! It's Peter. Let me in, quick!"

Rhoda was so relieved when she heard Peter's voice that she ran back into the house to tell the others that Peter had escaped. But in her excitement she forgot to open the door! The others didn't believe her at first. But Peter went on knocking at the door and at last they let him in.

After that, Peter escaped from Jerusalem and found somewhere else where he could carry on telling people about Jesus.

What else in God's big story links up with this?

**Escape by Earthquake!**
p. 248

# Paul Begins His Mission

A few years had passed since Jesus had appeared to Saul on the road to Damascus. Now Saul was working with an apostle called Barnabas in the city of Antioch, in Syria. Antioch was one of the largest cities in the empire. People from many different nations came to live there. The church in Antioch was growing bigger and stronger. (Other people noticed, and it was here in Antioch that the Jesus-followers were first called "Christians".) Saul and Barnabas loved to see how God was bringing all sorts of people into a single family. All that mattered was believing in Jesus.

Saul and Barnabas had worked together in Antioch for about a year, when God told them it was time to move on. It was around then that Saul decided to use his Greek name, "Paul". They got on a ship to Cyprus, and from there they sailed to Galatia. They went to the synagogues (the Judean assemblies) and explained that God had sent Israel's true king at last. This meant that Jesus was now Lord of the whole world, not just of the Judeans. Many of the Galatians believed their message, but some didn't like what they heard and they attacked Paul and Barnabas.

A little later, back in Antioch, the church had become alarmed and upset. Teachers from the church in Jerusalem had arrived, saying that only Judean people could be proper Jesus-followers. They said that if people from different nations wanted to join the church, they would have to follow the rules in the Law of Moses. At first, Peter himself was taken in by this. Even Barnabas agreed. But Paul knew it was wrong. He explained to Peter that when people who weren't Judeans joined a church, that didn't mean they had to start following the Law of Moses. Jesus' death had dealt with their sin, so how could they be seen as outsiders? Believing in Jesus and following his teaching was all that now mattered.

Later Paul wrote to the churches in Galatia to explain it all to them.

# An Important Meeting

Where's this in the Bible?

Acts 15

The teachers from Jerusalem had upset the church in Antioch by saying that everyone had to follow the Law of Moses. People were so disturbed by this that the leaders of the church decided to send Paul and Barnabas to Jerusalem to sort out the problem.

When they arrived in Jerusalem, Paul and Barnabas went straight to meet with the leaders of the church. Paul and Barnabas told them about their mission in Galatia, and how so many people who were not Judeans now believed in Jesus. They told them how God's Holy Spirit had acted powerfully for them, how lots of people had been healed, and how they had stopped worshipping idols and were worshipping God instead.

Peter was at the meeting. He had been listening carefully to everything Paul and Barnabas had said. He had also been thinking about what Paul had said to him at Antioch. And now he got up to speak. Peter explained to everyone what God had taught him when he visited Cornelius, and how the Roman soldier's whole family had been baptized by the Holy Spirit. "Now I understand," he said, "that God is telling us to welcome people from every nation into his family. They don't have to change who they are and follow the Law of Moses. All that matters is to believe and follow Jesus."

Then James, the brother of Jesus, pointed out that in the Bible the prophets had promised that one day people from all over the world would join God's people. And now that promise was coming true!

The meeting went on for a long time, but at last they reached agreement. They decided to write a letter to all the churches, telling them not to be alarmed or upset. All that mattered was that people should believe in Jesus and live the way that he wanted.

What else in God's big story links up with this?

**Peter Has a Vision**
p. 240

# Escape by Earthquake!

Where's this in the Bible?

Acts 16

Paul had found a new travelling companion. His name was Silas. They invited a young man called Timothy to join them. Timothy came from Galatia; everyone in his church spoke well of him.

The three companions sailed over to Greece and arrived in the city of Philippi. Paul began to teach people about Jesus. God's Spirit was with him and he healed people who were troubled in mind or body, showing them what powerful acts could be done in the name of Jesus. But some people didn't like what Paul was saying and they complained to the local rulers. The rulers ordered Paul and Silas to be beaten and thrown into prison.

While they were in the prison, Paul and Silas kept their spirits up by praying and singing hymns. They had been singing all that night, when suddenly the ground under them started to move and there was a great earthquake! The doors of the prison burst open and all the prisoners' chains fell off. The jailer was terrified that the prisoners would escape and he would be punished for letting them get away. But Paul shouted out, "Don't worry! We're all still here!"

The jailer called for lights and rushed in. Trembling all over, he fell down before Paul and Silas. "Sirs," he said, "please tell me how I can get out of this mess."

Paul replied, "Believe in the Lord Jesus, and you will be rescued." He did just that, and the jailer and his whole family were baptized that very day.

The next morning, the local rulers tried to send Paul and his friends away secretly. But Paul told the rulers they had been wrong to beat them and put them in prison, and he got them to apologize. Timothy learned a lot on that trip.

What else in God's big story links up with this?

**God Rescues Peter from Prison**
p. 242

# Learning to Love and Hope

Where's this
in the Bible?

1 Thessalonians

Thessalonica was a big city by the sea in Greece. When Paul went there and taught people about Jesus, many believed in him. But some people made trouble and forced Paul to leave town in a hurry. He made his way to Athens, and from there he wrote a letter to the Christians in Thessalonica.

In his letter, Paul explained that when you follow Jesus, some people will be angry and make trouble. Jesus himself suffered, and his followers will sometimes have to suffer too. But Paul was thrilled that the new Christians were standing firm in their faith despite their troubles. He urged them to live in the way God wanted, and to work hard so there would be enough money to care for poor people who needed it.

In Paul's first letter to the Thessalonians, he wrote this prayer:

"May God make your love for one another, and for everyone, grow bigger and overflow. That way, your hearts will be strengthened and kept blameless before God when our Lord Jesus is with us again."

The Thessalonians knew that one day Jesus would come back to be with them. But they were anxious about people who had already died. What would happen to them? How could they be with Jesus if they were dead?

Paul comforted them. He explained that when Jesus came back, all his people would be raised from the dead to share in God's new world. Nobody knew when Jesus would return, so they had to be ready. They had to live as though Jesus would come back at any moment!

What else in God's big story
links up with this?

**The Meaning of
Christian Love**
p. 254

# Paul Teaches in Athens

Where's this in the Bible?

Acts 17

Wherever Paul went, he would tell people that God had raised Jesus from the dead. Jesus was now the Lord of the whole world! One day, he would come back to the world and put everything right.

While Paul was staying in Athens, he told people about Jesus' "resurrection" (a word that means "standing up again"). But the people of Athens thought the words "Jesus" and "Resurrection" sounded like the names of a god and a goddess, and they didn't want any strange new gods brought into their city. They had enough gods and goddesses already, including their own goddess, Athene, after whom their city was named. So the Athenians took Paul to their supreme court in the middle of the city. There Paul told the Athenian judges about the one true God who had made the world. This is what he said:

"The God who made the world and everything in it, the Lord of heaven and earth, doesn't live in temples made by human hands. Nor does he need looking after by humans, since he himself is as close to us as breathing. In him we live and move and exist. As some of your own poets have said, 'We are his offspring.'

"Well, then, if we really are God's offspring, we ought not to think of God as an idol formed from metal or stone. That was just ignorance. Now God wants everyone to reject idols and worship him alone. God also wants you to know that he has set a day when he will judge the whole world by the man he has appointed. How do we know? Because he raised that man, Jesus, from the dead!"

When they heard that, lots of the Athenian judges just laughed. But some believed. And this time Paul wasn't punished for his dangerous teaching.

# The Meaning of Christian Love

Where's this
in the Bible?

1 Corinthians,
Galatians 3

Corinth was a busy city on the coast of Greece. It had a bustling seaport and market. When Paul visited Corinth, all sorts of people believed what he said. People from many different nations joined the new family of Jesus-followers, including lots of Judeans who lived in the city. The Judeans were excited to learn that Jesus was their true king, while lots of other people were thrilled to be equal members in the new family that God was creating.

Paul always tried to make it clear that all members of the church were the same in the eyes of God. It didn't matter whether they were Judean or not, whether they were male or female, rich or poor, slaves or free: everyone was equal. But there were some in the Corinthian church who hadn't fully accepted Paul's teaching, especially some of the wealthy members. They didn't want to worship alongside the poor, and certainly not with slaves. So, after Paul had moved on, he wrote a long letter to explain that everyone was equally important to God, and that they must worship together instead of splitting up into different groups. They also had to stop behaving in the selfish way they used to before they knew Jesus.

Paul knew that, above everything else, they had to learn that loving Jesus meant loving one another too, even people they used to look down on as different from themselves. This is what Paul wrote:

"Love is big-hearted, love is kind, it's never jealous, it isn't full of its own importance, it doesn't always try to get its own way, it doesn't get in a rage or bear a grudge, it doesn't take pleasure in others' harm, but rejoices in the truth."

Then, to sum up, Paul wrote, "Faith, hope, and love are the things that really matter. But the greatest thing of all is love."

What else in God's big story
links up with this?

**God is Love**
p. 274

# New Temple, New Thinking

Where's this in the Bible?

Acts 19, Ephesians; Philippians; Colossians

The apostle Paul never stopped telling the world about Jesus. Lots of people listened to him eagerly, but there were others who would do anything to stop him. Once, when Paul was in Ephesus, a city in Greece, some men who made statues of the goddess Artemis stirred up the whole city against him. A large angry crowd shouted for Paul to be killed, and the local rulers arrested him for causing a riot. A while later, Paul was put in prison for a long time, waiting to hear whether he would be released or put on trial. Some of his loyal friends came to visit him. They brought him news about the new churches he had started in towns and cities throughout the Roman Empire. All Paul could think of was how he could help the churches, and as he couldn't help them in person, he wrote them letters instead.

In his letters, Paul told the new churches that God had always planned to bring heaven and earth together, and that's what had happened in Jesus. When you believed in Jesus, you were believing in God himself, because God had revealed himself perfectly and completely in Jesus. In the past, God had been present in the Temple in Jerusalem, but now God was present in the new family of Jesus-followers, and they would be his Temple. Paul wrote in one letter:

"You are like the stones that are used to build a wonderful temple, with Jesus himself as the foundation stone. Each one of you is being fitted together, making a holy place where God will live by his Spirit."

This meant that Jesus' followers were to live as a single family, and to follow the way of holiness and purity. That way all the world would see that the true God was at work.

Paul couldn't possibly write down everything he wanted to say. So he tried to teach people to think things through for themselves, praying and trusting the Holy Spirit to guide them.

What else in God's big story links up with this?

**The Church is Born**
p. 232

# The Runaway Slave

Where's this in the Bible?

Philemon

While Paul was in prison, a young man came to him asking for help. His name was Onesimus, which means "useful". He was a slave, but he had run away from his master. In those days, wealthy Romans normally had several slaves in their households. One of these wealthy Christians was Philemon, the master of Onesimus.

Philemon was Paul's friend. It was thanks to Paul that he had come to know Jesus. And now, here was Philemon's slave asking for Paul's help! What was Paul to do? Roman law said that Paul should send him back. But Paul knew that Onesimus might be punished. He might even be killed.

So Paul wrote a letter to his friend, Philemon, and persuaded Onesimus to take it to his master. In the letter, Paul said:

"Onesimus has become like a child to me. And he loves Jesus too! So I want you to welcome him back in just the same way as you would welcome me. And perhaps you'll go one step further, and set him free? If he's done anything wrong, blame me instead.

"Oh, and by the way," wrote Paul, "when I get out of prison I'll come and visit you. I'm looking forward to seeing how you're all getting on."

# Paul Explains God's Plan

Where's this in the Bible?

Romans

Some time later, after he had been released from prison, Paul made plans to go to Rome, the capital city of the empire. After that, he planned to go to Spain. But first, he decided to write a long letter to the churches in Rome. In his letter, Paul explained that the good news of Jesus' resurrection showed what God had been planning from the very beginning. He reminded them how, long ago, God had made a special agreement with Abraham, saying, "I will make you the father of a great nation, and through you I will bless all the families in the whole world."

Paul explained how God was fulfilling that promise by blessing all people through Jesus, forgiving their sins, and bringing them into his family. This message was for everybody. God had put the world right through Jesus, and when people believed in Jesus they, too, would be put right. And they would become part of God's plan for his new world.

Paul told them that becoming a Christian didn't mean life would become easy, but that God's love would always be with them, no matter what might happen to them. This is how he put it in his letter:

"The sufferings we go through in the present time aren't worth comparing with the glory that is going to be revealed for us. The whole world is on tiptoe with expectation, eagerly awaiting the moment when heaven and earth will come together and God's children will be revealed."

Paul knew that his own people, the Judeans, often found this message difficult. So he explained that Jesus really was their long-awaited leader, the true king that God had promised to send. That's why all Christians, including those from Judea, had to worship together as a single family. It would be a sign to the world that Jesus was Lord, and that God's new world was beginning.

## What else in God's big story links up with this?

**God Makes a Special Agreement**
p. 18

**Jesus Rises from the Dead**
p. 220

# Paul Causes a Riot

Where's this in the Bible?

Acts 21–25

Paul had planned to go to Rome, but first he had to go back to Jerusalem. But when he was there, some Judeans who didn't believe in Jesus spotted Paul and seized him. "Men of Israel," they yelled, "come and help us! This is the man who's been turning everyone against our people, our Law, and our Temple!" An angry crowd gathered and soon Paul was being dragged along and beaten. News of the disturbance reached the army, and soldiers were sent to arrest Paul and take him away. But the crowd ran after the soldiers and closed in on them, shouting, "Kill him! Kill him!"

After his arrest, Paul was put on trial before the Judean council. When it was time for him to speak, Paul stood up and declared, "I'm here because of my hope in the resurrection of the dead!" Some members of the council believed in resurrection, but others didn't, and they ended up arguing among themselves. They couldn't agree on what should be done, so the trial had to be stopped, and Paul was taken back to prison. The next morning Paul woke up to find someone waiting to see him with an urgent message. It was Paul's nephew, who lived in Jerusalem. "Uncle Paul," he said, "you're in grave danger. I've heard that some trouble-makers are plotting to capture you, and they intend to kill you!"

Paul told his nephew to find the Roman officer in charge of the prison and tell him about the plot. "I'm not having that!" said the officer, and he ordered a large squad of soldiers to take Paul away at the dead of night. They took him to the city of Caesarea, well away from Jerusalem. While Paul was there, the Roman governor decided to question him. But Paul could tell that the governor was really trying to trick him, so Paul said, "I've had enough of this. As a Roman citizen, I have the right to be tried by the Emperor!" That meant he would have to be taken to Rome, which was where Paul had been planning to go all along.

# Shipwreck!

Where's this in the Bible?

Acts 27–28

At last, Paul's journey to Rome had begun. Still tied in chains, he boarded a ship, accompanied by a small group of Roman soldiers who were guarding him. A few friends also went with him.

The ship sailed past Cyprus and on toward Crete, where the ship's crew tried to find a port where they could spend the winter. But a strong wind blew them into a stormy sea, and they were tossed back and forth by the waves. As Paul said his prayers, an angel spoke to him. "Don't be afraid, Paul," said the angel. "You will get to Rome, and God will look after everyone on board, too."

One morning, after two weeks of being blown about by the storm, Paul and his friends saw in the distance a rocky island. The waves were driving the ship toward it! With a loud CRASH, the ship smashed into the rocks and broke into pieces. Everyone had to swim for shore, or paddle on bits of wood. But they all got safely to land.

The island, they discovered, was Malta. The local people were kind and looked after them. When they found out that Paul could heal people in the name of Jesus, many of them came to him to be cured.

After winter was over, Paul and his friends found a ship sailing to Italy. It arrived in the south of Italy, and Paul and his companions finished the journey on foot. When Paul finally reached Rome, lots of Christians were waiting there to greet him. They had received his letter and now they were overjoyed to see him in person.

# Paul in Rome

Where's this in the Bible?

Act 28

In Rome, Paul was allowed to rent a house, as long as he was guarded by a soldier. He was waiting for his trial before the Emperor.

Paul was anxious to meet the Judeans who lived in Rome who hadn't become Christians. Many of the Judeans who still lived in Judea wanted to rebel and fight against Rome. Paul was worried that the Judeans in Rome might think that he was going to tell the Emperor that they were planning to rebel as well. After all, some Judeans had treated Paul very badly. Paul wanted to make it clear that he wasn't out to get his own back.

So Paul invited the Judean leaders in Rome for a discussion. They studied the Bible together and talked from morning to night. Paul explained how everything that God had promised to Abraham, and everything in the Law of Moses and the prophets, had come true in Jesus. Paul wanted them to see that Jesus was God's answer to all their hopes and prayers. He said to them, "I'm a prisoner because I share the same hope as you, not because I'm rejecting it!"

Some of the Judean leaders believed what Paul told them about Jesus, but others didn't. That made Paul sad. He reminded them that the prophets had said that one day some of God's people would refuse to listen and would stop believing altogether.

Paul lived under guard in his house in Rome for another two years, waiting for his trial. During that time he received lots of visitors. He taught them that Jesus was God's true king, and that he was now Lord of the world. Nobody tried to stop him.

# God's New Agreement

Where's this in the Bible?

Hebrews

Around that time, another Christian leader wrote an important letter. Like Paul's letters, it was full of teaching that would help the new churches understand what it means to be a follower of Jesus. This particular letter was written to some Judean Christians who were clinging to the special agreement that God had made at the time of Moses. They were hoping that somehow they could carry on doing everything laid down in the Law of Moses, even the sacrifices in the Temple, while also following Jesus.

The letter explained that, long ago, the prophet Jeremiah had said that one day God would make a new agreement with his people. And now, thanks to Jesus, that new agreement had begun! This meant that lots of the old ways had to change. Through Jesus, God was making a fresh start. It was the beginning of a whole new world! This is what the letter said:

"You have to go forward into God's new plan, not backwards to the old one. Jesus sacrificed himself for us on the cross, so there's no longer any need to sacrifice animals. We don't need lots of priests to sacrifice the animals, either! Jesus himself is our Great High Priest. This means we can now pray to God through him, and have faith that God hears us.

"All the great men and women in the Bible were people of faith: Abel, Noah, Abraham, Sarah, Isaac, Jacob, Joseph, Moses, Rahab, Gideon, Samson, David, Samuel, and all the prophets. All of them lived by faith. We have to be like them, keeping faith in God and his promises, and always looking to Jesus as our leader."

THE NEW TESTAMENT

What else in God's big story links up with this?

**Sin and Forgiveness**
p. 50

**God Promises to Rescue His People**
p. 118

# Wisdom for a New World

Where's this in the Bible?

James

James was the brother of Jesus. After Jesus had gone to be with God in heaven, James became the leader of the church in Jerusalem. He wrote a letter to Jesus' followers to encourage them at a difficult time. In his letter, James said many things that echoed what Jesus himself had said:

"Everyone should be quick to hear, slow to speak, slow to anger. Human anger, you see, doesn't produce God's justice! So put away everything that is bad and sinful, and take to your hearts the word of God which has been planted inside you and which has the power to rescue you."

James wrote that it wasn't enough just to say that you believed in God. There had to be a real change in how you behaved as well, especially in the way you looked after people in need. He pointed out that rich people are often cruel and hurtful to the poor. It was, after all, rich people who sent Jesus to his death. James warned that the words we say matter more than we might think. The tongue, he said, is like a fire that can set things ablaze. Or it's like a wild animal looking for someone to bite. We have to learn how to tame it!

James wrote that there are two kinds of wisdom. One is false, and comes from people who are cunning, jealous, boastful, and tell lies. The other is true, and comes from people who are humble, holy, gentle, kind, and sincere. This is the wisdom of God's new world.

James ended his letter by encouraging everyone, always, to be patient, to pray, and to trust God for everything.

What else in God's big story links up with this?

**Wisdom for Life**
p. 90

**Jesus Teaches People about God**
p. 162

THE NEW TESTAMENT

270

# Trusting in God

Where's this in the Bible?

1 Peter

The apostle Peter also wrote letters to the new churches. While Jesus was on earth, Peter had been right there with him. He had seen Jesus suffer and die. And he remembered how Jesus had told him that to follow Jesus would mean suffering as well. But now, many followers of Jesus were alarmed when people hated them and made them suffer for their faith. They worried that everything was going wrong.

"No," wrote Peter in a letter. "Your faith is like gold. Gold is tested by fire to see if it's the real thing. That's what it's like when you suffer for believing in Jesus. Your faith is being tested."

Peter said that the way to deal with suffering was always to remember Jesus:

"He committed no sin, nor were there any lies in his mouth. When he was insulted, he didn't insult anyone in return. When he suffered, he didn't threaten. He himself carried our sins in his body on the cross. It is by his wounds that you are healed. For you were going astray like sheep, but now you have returned to the shepherd and guardian of your true lives."

Later, toward the end of his letter, Peter wrote:

"Stay awake! Your enemy, the devil, is roaming around like a roaring lion, looking for someone to eat. Don't give in to him, but stay faithful to God. Then, after you have suffered a little while, God himself will put everything right."

What else in God's big story links up with this?

**Jesus and the Big Storm**
p. 172

**The Suffering Servant**
p. 120

# God is Love

Where's this
in the Bible?

1 John

The apostle John knew that what mattered, above everything else, was love. God loved us so much that he sent his son, Jesus, to die for us. And love was at the heart of everything Jesus himself had taught. That was what John wanted to remind everyone about when he wrote his first letter. This is what he said:

"If we love one another, God lives in us and his love is completed in us. God is love. Those who live in love live in God, and God lives in them. There is no fear in love, but complete love drives out fear. Fear has to do with punishment, and anyone who is afraid hasn't been completed in love."

John went on to say that it's no good saying "I love God" if we hate a brother or sister, if we're always angry with them or picking fights with them. Anyone who loves God should love everyone in their family too.

Loving God means doing what he says. When we live like that, we share in the victory that Jesus has won. Evil won't have the last word! Our faith will win the day.

When we believe and love like that, we can pray confidently. God will hear us when we ask him for things. When we learn what pleases him, we can ask for it, and we know he will give it to us.

What else in God's big story
links up with this?

**Jesus Teaches
People about God**
p. 162

**Jesus is Crucified**
p. 216

# John's Vision of Jesus

Where's this in the Bible?

Revelation 1

A prophet called John was telling people that Jesus was the Lord and Saviour of the world. But at that time the rulers of the Roman Empire were saying that the Emperor was "Lord" and "Saviour"! So when they found out about John, they arrested him and banished him to a little island called Patmos.

John prayed and prayed to God, and one Sunday morning he had a vision. God's Holy Spirit helped him to hear and see Jesus himself!

In the vision, Jesus was wearing a long robe, with a golden belt. His head and his hair were white like snow. His eyes were like fire. His feet were like polished brass. His voice was like a waterfall. He was so bright that seeing him was like looking straight at the midday sun!

When John saw Jesus like this, he fell down to the ground as if he were dead. But Jesus touched him. "Don't be afraid," he said. "I am the first and the last. I am the living one. I was dead. But look! I am alive forever and ever.

"Now write what you see, both the things that are already happening, and also the things that are going to happen afterwards."

And that is just what John did.

What else in God's big story links up with this?

**Isaiah's Vision of Yahweh**
p. 104

**On the Road to Damascus**
p. 238

THE NEW TESTAMENT

276

# A Song for Everyone!

Where's this
in the Bible?

Revelation 4–5

While he was living on the island of Patmos, John saw many visions. In one of them, he was shown what is happening in heaven all the time. He saw a majestic person sitting on a glorious throne, with 24 "elders" all around, standing for the whole people of God. Four mysterious creatures were there too. The first looked like a lion, the second was like an ox, the third had a human face, and the fourth was like a flying eagle. They were singing a hymn of praise to the person on the throne:

"Holy, holy, holy, Lord God Almighty, who was and is and is to come.
You made all things the way you intended them to be."

The person on the throne had a scroll, but nobody could open it. Then one of the elders said, "The Lion of Judah has won! He can open the scroll." John looked, and near the throne he saw, not a lion, but a lamb! It had been killed, but it was now standing up again. The lamb took the scroll. Then everyone around the throne sang a new song:

"You can take the scroll.
You can read what it says.
By your death you bought people for God
From every tribe and nation,
And made them a kingdom and priests to our God
And they will reign on the earth."

Everybody joined in, praising God and the Lamb.

What else in God's big story
links up with this?

**Isaiah's Vision
of Yahweh**
p. 104

**God Abandons
the Temple**
p. 110

THE NEW TESTAMENT

# New Heaven, New Earth

Where's this
in the Bible?

Revelation 21–22

In his final vision, John saw what was going to happen at the end of time. He saw a new heaven and a new earth. He saw a beautiful city, the heavenly Jerusalem, coming down to earth from heaven. And he heard a loud voice that declared, "God has come to live with humans! He will wipe away every tear from their eyes. There will be no more death, or crying, or pain." God was making everything new.

The heavenly Jerusalem looked like a bride dressed up for her husband. At last heaven and earth were joined, and they would be married forever! The heavenly Jerusalem was where God's plan for his world would come true. As John said:

"I saw no Temple in the city, because the Lord God Almighty is its Temple. And the city has no need of sun or moon to shine on it, for the glory of God gives it light. The nations will walk in its light, and the kings of the earth will bring their glory into it."

Then John saw something else that made him wide-eyed with wonder.

"After that, I saw the river of the Water of Life. It was sparkling like crystal, and flowing from the throne of God through the middle of the street of the city. On either bank of the river was growing the Tree of Life, and the leaves of the tree are for the healing of the nations."

All this would happen when Jesus returned to complete his reign. So John's final prayer was, "Yes! Come soon, Lord Jesus!"

What else in God's big story links up with this?

**The Garden of Eden**
p. 4

**The Promise of a New World**
p. 132

# Jesus, the New Beginning

Where's this
in the Bible?

John 1

In the beginning was God's Word, and the Word was God.
All things were made through him.
True life, and true light, were in him, coming into the world.
The light shines in the darkness
And the darkness hasn't overcome it.

God's Word was in the world, the world that he made,
but the world didn't know him.
He came to his own people,
and his own people didn't accept him.
But to all who did accept him, and believed in him,
he gave the right to become God's children.

God's Word became flesh and came to live among us.
We gazed on his glory, the glory of the Father's only Son,
full of God's kindness and truth.
The Law was given through Moses.
God's kindness and truth came through Jesus.

Nobody has ever seen God.
God the only Son, who is close to the Father's heart,
He has shown us who God really is.

What else in God's big story
links up with this?

**What are Humans?**
p. 6

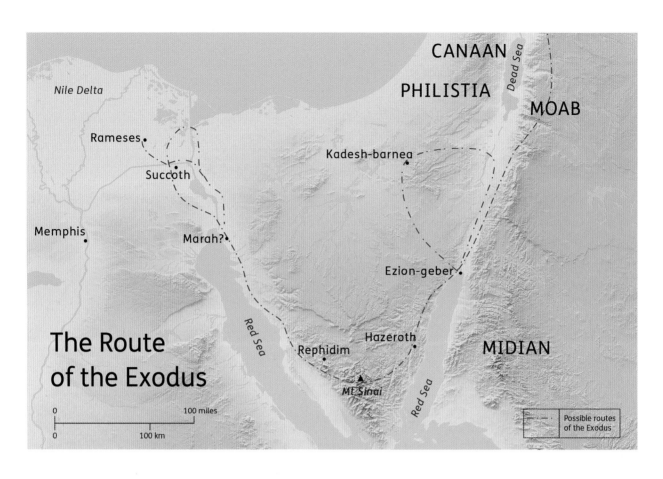

The Route
of the Exodus

Possible routes
of the Exodus

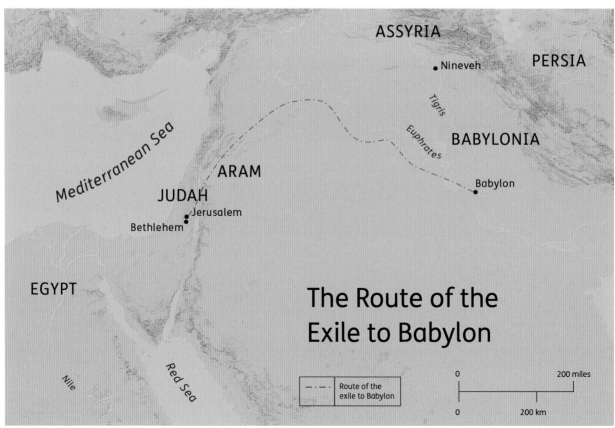

The Route of the
Exile to Babylon

Route of the
exile to Babylon

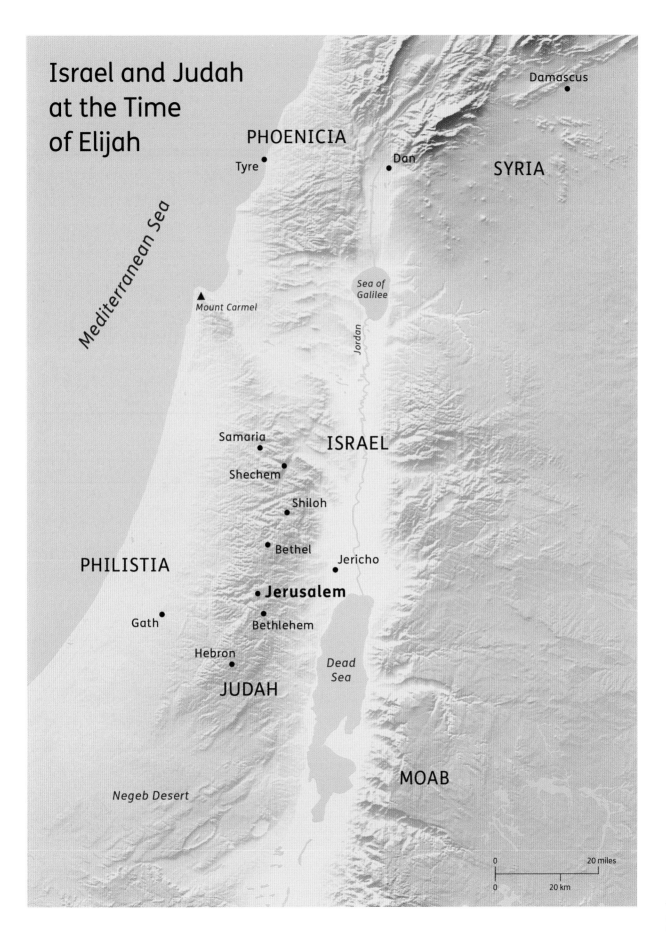

Israel and Judah
at the Time
of Elijah

PHOENICIA

Tyre

Damascus

Dan

SYRIA

Mediterranean Sea

Mount Carmel

Sea of
Galilee

Jordan

Samaria

ISRAEL

Shechem

Shiloh

Bethel

Jericho

PHILISTIA

**Jerusalem**

Gath

Bethlehem

Hebron

Dead
Sea

JUDAH

MOAB

Negeb Desert

0          20 miles

0      20 km

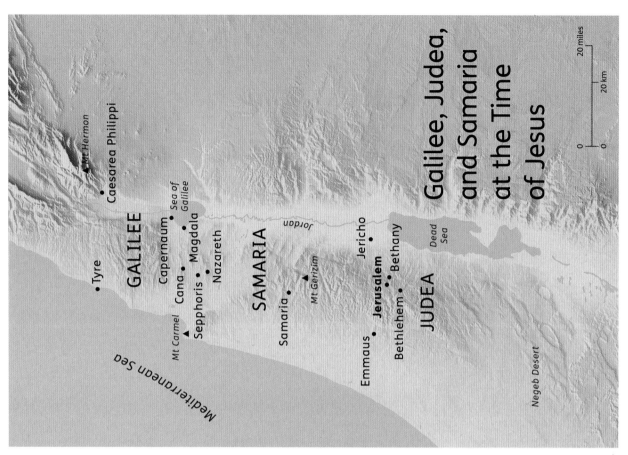

Galilee, Judea, and Samaria at the Time of Jesus

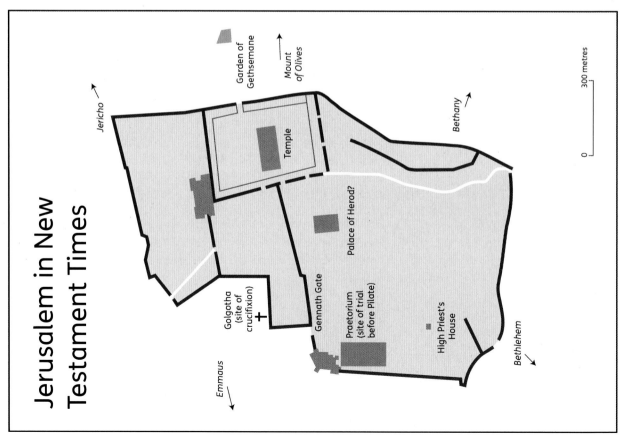

Jerusalem in New Testament Times

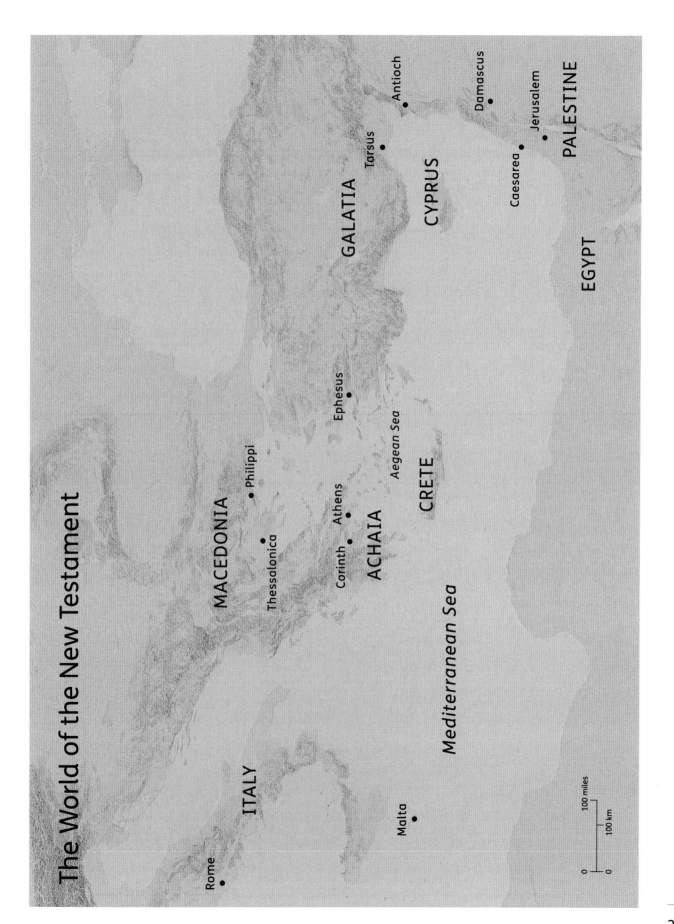

# The World of the New Testament

Rome

ITALY

MACEDONIA

Philippi

Thessalonica

Corinth

Athens

ACHAIA

Ephesus

Aegean Sea

CRETE

GALATIA

Tarsus

CYPRUS

Antioch

Damascus

Jerusalem

Caesarea

PALESTINE

EGYPT

Malta

Mediterranean Sea

| 0 | 100 miles |
| 0 | 100 km |

# Index

289